Understanding the Senior Adult

A Tool for Wholistic Ministry

LOIS D. KNUTSON

FOREWORD BY MELVIN A. KIMBLE

An Alban Institute Publication

Library of Congress Catalog Card Number 99-73549
ISBN 1-56699-217-6

CONTENTS

FOREWORD

Lois Knutson conveys an uncommon breadth and depth of gerontological knowledge and pastoral insight in this helpful, comprehensive book for congregational wholistic ministry with older adults. This unabashedly "how to" book for developing a well-coordinated ministry identifies critical themes and issues that confront older adults and their families.

Knutson reminds us that older adults compose one of the most significant groups of people that pastors and the faith community are called upon to nurture. Although older persons constitute 12.7 percent of our society, most Christian denominations in the United States report that persons over the age of 65 make up more than 20 to 25 percent of their membership. It is estimated that more than half of a pastor's ministry is directly related to older persons and their families. Clergy and their congregations are obviously in a perfect position to respond to the needs and challenges of the aged and their families. By providing such ministry they also have an unique opportunity to be facilitators and enablers of parish and community programs that serve older adults.

Knutson reminds us that aging touches all of the basic questions of life. The biomedical paradigm that has dominated gerontology since its beginning has outlived its usefulness and needs to be replaced by a paradigm with a wider frame of reference if the full range of questions evoked by the human phenomenon of aging are to be examined. It is a whole person with spiritual, psychosocial, physical, and emotional dimensions who is aging and aged. An effective model for responsible congregational ministry will seek to encompass all these dimensions.

We need to remember that although aging is largely a positive experience for most persons, it is unpredictable and unique for everyone. Many variables shape and determine health and quality of life. With all of our individual uniqueness and diversity, however, we have opportunities for spiritual development and growth to the very end. With the dramatic increase in the longevity of older adults comes an increase not only in their numbers but also in their potential for spiritual growth and discovery of spiritual truths.

The task of providing wholistic ministry with senior adults begins with a comprehensive view of life that is neither escapist or evasive but confronts life with all of its fullness as well as its limitations. The faith community becomes a vessel of that care as it participates with people in those pivotal events at every stage of the human life cycle. The theological and biblical resources for ministry and for the expression of the caring community are made visible in the congregation where the whole family of God is gathered. In such a supportive atmosphere, strengths and weaknesses, joys and sorrows, and talents and limitations are shared. Ministry presents the challenge of being a faithful guide and supportive resource to people in their quest for wholeness, grace, and meaning in all stages of life, including old age.

The challenge of older adulthood is to make sense of life at a stage where losses and changes occur with bewildering and sometimes overwhelming frequency and intensity. As a covenant community of believers, the church is the source and center of the ultimate meaning of life and the proclamation of the gospel. Older persons need purpose in order to continue to struggle with the eroding and debilitating diminishments that aging and growing old introduce. In a society that measures life in ways that often devalue and dehumanize, the gospel with its recreative power presents Christians at whatever stage of life with a destiny and a purpose.

In a congregational ministry with older adults that seeks to be comprehensive many opportunities for pastoral care and congregational services will surface. Knutson, for example, recognizes that grief is a common denominator of life. Responding to unresolved grief may be one of the most helpful and healing ministries that pastors and the community of believers can provide. Older persons need supportive settings and relationships for dealing with the many grief issues that make up their lives. In a Christian community, a person should never have to fear dying in isolation or alone. The church must strive to be a caring, nurturing community that comforts those who mourn and tends to those who are dying. Such ministry demands both skill and faithfulness, and must always be a priority in the midst of all the demands on the pastor's or other caregiver's time and presence. Knutson presents a model for pastoral ministry to help spiritually prepare older adults for death.

Writing out of her nearly two decades of parish ministry and chaplaincy service, Knutson provides a landmark model for doing senior adult wholistic ministry. At the center of her model is a comprehensive Parish Spiritual Assessment Tool as well as a Spiritual Journey Exercise for Individuals. The assessment tools she introduces probe not only the spiritual dimensions of life but examine such topics as the psychological aspects of aging, senior adults-family dynamics, economic and societal influences on aging, as well as a medical overview.

As we move into the next millennium, few roadmaps chart the new territories introduced by the increased life expectancy of older persons. Older adults are not a homogenous population. Even though future cohorts of older adults will be healthier, better educated, and increasingly active, there will remain a large number of frail older adults for whom the need for care doubles every five years after the age of 65. Because of the large percentage of elderly who are members of the church and participate in congregational life, the church has a unique opportunity to support them in a quest for wholeness that enlarges and enriches their experience of grace and meaning in this last stage of life.

This is an engaging and comprehensive volume for doing pastoral ministry with older adults and promises to be instrumental in widening the horizons of all who engage in congregational ministry with older adults. Because the author is intending for this book to be used as a programmatic manual, her spiritual assessment tools with instructions on how to implement them will prove most helpful to pastors and laity.

I am proud to claim Lois Knutson as a former student in my classes at Luther Seminary and also as a graduate of the Geriatric Pastoral Care Institute of the Center for Aging, Religion and Spirituality. Her stature as a pastoral practitioner who knows the theory and praxis of gerontological ministry is underscored by this important book. I regard this book as a welcome contribution to the growing body of literature on gerontological congregational pastoral care ministry.

As I reflect on my own aging, underscored by my new professional title of emeritus professor, and begin to envision my own older adult life, I would wish and pray that my pastor and faith community might reflect some of the same sensitivity and insight displayed in this volume concerning my spiritual needs and other challenges and changes I will inevitably face on my spiritual journey of aging.

I enthusiastically welcome this book as an important contribution to the increasing body of literature on pastoral care with the aging.

Melvin A. Kimble
Emeritus Professor of Pastoral Care and
Director of the Center
for Aging, Religion and Spirituality
Luther Seminary
St. Paul, Minnesota

PREFACE

This book is about loving the elderly. My love for the elderly began with my maternal grandparents, who lived a block and a half from my childhood home. They were my baptismal sponsors, role models of faith, teachers of creation and life experiences, and confidants. We grew older together. Today my love for the elderly continues as my mother ages. She is not only my mother but also my best friend and role model. We are blessed that we can grow older together. As my call to geriatric ministry evolved through my grandparents and my mother, it naturally extended to the senior adult parishioners, residents, and patients whom I have served in 18 years of ordained ministry.

Why a book about ministry with senior adults? They are the mainstay of a congregation's membership. Many older people serve as models of faithful worship attendance and participation in Holy Communion. Many read their Bibles at home regularly and participate in congregational Bible study when they are able. Some seniors serve God's people by making quilts, preparing meals for funerals, singing in the choir, joining a prayer chain, visiting the homebound, participating in women's and men's organizations, volunteering in the church office, and working with the senior advisory committee. For many aging men and women, sacrificial financial stewardship is part of a Christian lifestyle. Senior adults often serve as exemplars of the godly life.

Just as national statistics indicate that the older-adult population is increasing rapidly, so too the percentage of elderly members in congregations is on the rise. Just as congregations have structured ministry for children and youth, evangelism, worship and music, stewardship, social outreach, and Christian education, a structured program is also needed, I believe, for ministry with senior adults. Aging members should not be given the leftover time on the congregation's and pastor's schedule.

This is a how-to book for developing a structured and well-coordinated program for senior adult ministry. The program puts pastors and lay caregivers at the cutting edge in ministry with the aging. It contains everything the reader needs to know to get a program up and running. The program structure applies the same goals of one-on-one visits with senior adults to the corporate congregational level of senior adult ministry. These goals include assisting older members to find meaning in life by discovering how God's love and presence connect with their past, present, and future experiences, and encouraging them to draw on inner strength and resources for hope.

Part I focuses on a Parish Spiritual Assessment Tool for one-on-one visits with senior adults. The older person visited by a pastor or lay caregiver who follows this format is likely to grow in faith, find renewed meaning in life, and experience divine peace. The caregiver who uses this tool will be motivated and invigorated to visit senior adults. The visitor will no longer wonder what to talk about, nor will she or he be perceived as only talking about the weather and drinking coffee. Chapter 1 describes the wholistic Parish Spiritual Assessment Tool (including spiritual, psychological, family, socioeconomic, and medical components). It advises caregivers how to use the assessment and plan process, which is essential to providing high-quality pastoral care with this format. This chapter includes the tool itself.

Part II includes a detailed chapter about each component of the tool (spiritual, psychological, family, socioeconomic, and medical). Each chapter begins with a composite story about a real life situation of senior adults. The story is followed by examples of age-related issues from one of the components. Laity will gain insight into their own aging process from these chapters. Each chapter closes by applying the assessment and plan process to the case described. Chapter 7 adapts the format to nursing home visits.

Part III shows congregations how to apply the goals of the Parish Spiritual Assessment Tool to the congregational level of senior adult ministry. Chapter 8 does just what every parish pastor resists: It proposes a new committee. In this case, however, forming a senior advisory committee ensures that senior adult ministry in the congregation is continually addressed. This chapter offers a guide to forming the committee, includes a sample committee job description and meeting agenda, and suggests ideas for congregational programs for senior adults.

Chapter 9 provides a congregation with the tools to observe an annual "Bless the Years" Sunday. This worship service affirms the dignity and worth of the elderly and assists younger members to relate to their elders in love. This chapter describes step-by-step planning and organization for the observance and includes bulletin content, a sample sermon, and a children's sermon. This chapter can be modified for use in long-term-care facilities.

Chapter 10 addresses holiday grief. The Christmas Service of Comfort and Remembrance can be used in congregations and long-term-care facilities that have mourned numerous deaths over the previous year, as well as by groupings of congregations for a community service. The chapter tells how to plan and organize the worship service and includes bulletin content and a sample sermon offering practical suggestions for dealing with holiday grief. This service can bring peace to those who are marking their first Christmas without a deceased relative or friend.

The "Blessing of the New Home" service in chapter 11 is an extension of the Nursing Home Spiritual Assessment Tool found in chapter 7. This liturgical service, held in the new residence of a senior adult (especially in a nursing home, assisted living facility, or other senior housing), calls forth from God, at a time of transition and adjustment, a special blessing on relocating elders, their families, and their new places of abode. The complete service is included, as well as detailed suggestions for use.

It is my conviction that senior adults, pastors, and congregations that develop a well-coordinated program of ministry with senior adults are blessed. This book offers a practical, intentional, and loving way to make that happen.

Packaged with the book is a CD-ROM for your convenience. The Parish Spiritual Assessment Tool is included on the CD-ROM so that caregivers can easily download the tool for record-keeping (the note-taking process is described in the book). Having the assessment tool on the disk makes it easy for readers to modify the tool for their own faith traditions. This is true also for the other items on the CD-ROM: Appendix A (Spiritual Journey Exercise for Individuals), the Nursing Home Spiritual Assessment Tool, the Bless the Years order of worship, the Christmas Service of Comfort and Remembrance order of worship, the Blessing the New Home Service liturgy, Appendix B (Internet Web Sites on Aging), plus two bonus items not included in the book: the Spiritual Journey Exercise for Small Groups and the Spiritual Journey Exercise for Confirmation Students.

The anecdotes in this book are composites derived from typical situations in the lives of senior adults. Any resemblance to actual events or persons is entirely coincidental and is not intended by the author.

ACKNOWLEDGMENTS

I am grateful to Our Savior's Lutheran Church of Montevideo, Minn., Luther Haven Nursing Home of Montevideo; and the Southwestern Minnesota Synod of the Evangelical Lutheran Church in America for their support of my participation in the two-year certificate program of the Geriatric Pastoral Care Institute of the Center for Aging, Religion, and Spirituality at Luther Seminary, St. Paul, Minn. This program was the impetus for my writing. I thank the CARS staff for exemplifying and encouraging a high standard of scholarship, as well as for living out a compassionate and loving spirituality for daily geriatric ministry.

I express deep thanks to the Rev. Douglas Olson of Our Savior's Lutheran Church for his ongoing enthusiastic support, as well as his zeal for creative ministry for senior adults in our congregation. I thank Dr. James Seeber of the CARS staff for his expertise in critiquing my project and encouraging me to develop it further, Dr. Susan McFadden of the CARS staff for her encouragement and expertise in critiquing parts of my Parish Spiritual Assessment Tool, my classmates at CARS for their feedback on my class project, the Association of Lutheran Older Adults, the Anderson Funeral Home of Montevideo, and all senior adults in all settings of my ministry who have shared their lives with me.

I extend special gratitude to Dr. Melvin Kimble–pastor, professor of geriatric ministry, and founder of the Center for Aging, Religion, and Spirituality–for graciously writing the foreword. Dr. Kimble is an exemplar of what he teaches: Possibilities abound for profound growth in late life; spiritual meaning endures forever.

I thank editor Beth Gaede and copyeditor Jean Lyles of the Alban Institute for their expert assistance in honing my writing skills and for their support of my manuscript.

Most of all, I thank my wise and loving mother, who has always said that I should write a book. Mom, this book is dedicated to you!

PART I

The Parish Spiritual Assessment Tool

CHAPTER 1

Meaningful Parish Visitation

Although spiritual assessments are sometimes required in health care settings, they are rarely used in parish ministry. Through my experience as both a parish pastor and a chaplain, I have discovered that conducting spiritual assessments with senior adults in the parish can deepen their faith experience and invigorate my ministry of visitation.

My interest in spiritual assessment began during clinical pastoral education as I experimented with integrating my assessment of the patient's spiritual, psychological, physical, and socioeconomic needs into a care plan for future visits. When I began my present parish position, I adapted the format to geriatric ministry. As visitation pastor for a congregation of 1,900 parishioners, of whom more than 500 are over 65, and as chaplain of a 120-bed nursing home, I expanded this spiritual assessment process into a time-efficient format for long-term relationships with senior adults in parish ministry. This approach is helpful to members and stimulating for me.

Through my participation in and completion of the two-year Geriatric Pastoral Care Institute program of the Center for Aging, Religion, and Spirituality at Luther Seminary in St. Paul, Minn., I was able to research many spiritual assessment tools, develop a well-defined theology of aging, integrate spiritual assessment with that theology, and adapt the process to long-term parish visitation with aged members (in contrast to my previous short-term relationships with hospital patients).

I use this Parish Spiritual Assessment Tool in all my visits with senior adults. It works, and it is easy to use, although to the reader initially perusing it, the tool may appear overwhelming. It is my experience that using the tool does not require a lot of time. In fact, it actually saves time! The key is to become familiar with it. During a visit, I use only the areas that apply specifically to the person at hand. This rewarding and enjoyable style of visiting has made a tremendous difference in my ministry. Not only am I able to offer senior adults a more meaningful perspective on life, but I find myself challenged to explore my own life more deeply.

The Parish Spiritual Assessment Tool includes these primary components: spiritual, psychological, family, socioeconomic, and medical, plus an assessment and plan process. It begins with the spiritual component because spiritual care is the calling of pastors. While the spiritual component as presented here is based on my Lutheran tradition, the tool can easily be adapted to any theological tradition. The spiritual component is foundational for visitation. The others are included because pastors know that psychological, family, socioeconomic, and medical concerns are intricately woven into the fabric of seniors' spiritual lives. Occasionally pastors need to become actively involved in these areas of members' lives. This tool offers a method to ascertain when to become involved and a plan to follow when doing so.

While this tool can greatly strengthen parish ministry with senior adults, it can also be adapted by others who visit aging people. It can be used by nursing home and hospital chaplains, Stephen ministers[1], assisted-living facility staff, nursing home staff, home health-care workers, hospice staff, lay visitors, families of senior adults, and confirmation adopt-a-grandparent programs (as found on the accompanying CD-ROM).

Goals of the Tool

The practical goals of the Parish Spiritual Assessment Tool are sixfold:

1. Senior adults will be assisted to find renewed meaning in life by discovering how God's love and presence connect with their past, present, and future experiences.

2. They will be encouraged to draw on inner strength and resources for daily and future hope.

3. While empathic pastoral care can help reduce stress and lead to self-awareness, a theological and wholistic assessment with this tool will lead the caregiver to identify, intervene, and help the member resolve lifelong and current issues.

4. This tool will encourage trusting relationships between caregivers and those whom they visit.

5. It will promote accountability and intentionality in visitation.

6. It will motivate and invigorate parish pastors to visit the homebound elderly, especially pastors who find such visits boring and believe they consume time best spent in other areas of ministry.

For effective use of the Parish Spiritual Assessment Tool it is essential that the pastor or other caregiver make use of the assessment and plan process at the end of each visit. This step is what makes the tool "work" for both senior adults and caregivers. Formulating a spiritual assessment and a plan for the follow-up visit allows the caregiver to see the larger issues in members' lives and not only the ever-changing daily issues. Seeing the forest as well as the trees in senior adults' lives is exciting for the pastor who enjoys integrating theology into daily life, and it is enlightening for aging members who seek spiritual nurture and growth. "Assessment" does not necessarily imply a problem. In fact, an assessment will often describe positive and deep spirituality.

Formulating the assessment and plan need not take more than five minutes. These minutes can save the caregiver time and anxiety later. On the follow-up visit, he or she will not spend time trying to remember what was discussed previously. In this sense, the process can be a boon to pastors and other caregivers. It is not unusual after a visit for a senior adult to say to a friend, "I had such a good visit with the pastor," not realizing that the "good visit" was due to the pastor's format for visitation using the Parish Spiritual Assessment Tool.

The assessment tool can be used either informally or formally. When it is used informally, caregivers will have such a working knowledge of it that they need not carry a printed copy of it into the visit. When the tool is used formally, the caregiver will bring along a copy. In either situation, this tool is not meant to override senior adults' own agendas. The visitor's primary agenda is the senior adult, who may have items of concern or interest to impart. Those items always take precedence over use of the tool.

Using the Tool Informally

Senior adult raises subject. When the homebound parishioner raises a subject for conversation, the visitor will respond accordingly and be able to focus on that topic in greater depth by using the discussion questions in the appropriate area of the assessment tool. For example, when the older member wants to talk about prayer (part IV of the spiritual component) and the spiritual component is used as a conversation guide, the member's preferred forms of prayer can be discussed, as well as other forms suggested in the tool. Following the order of the questions, the caregiver and the senior adult may choose to discuss possible difficulties with prayer, identifying (and dealing with) issues of concern by discussing what the member prays for, exploring the importance of prayer by inquiring about its frequency, and discussing how prayers are answered. A conversation about the person's view of God (part VI, spiritual component) may also ensue.

Caregiver initiates subject. When the pastor uses the assessment tool, she or he can initiate an informal spiritual and theological conversation based on what happens during the visit. For example, when the pastor brings communion to the home, the sacrament may take on deeper significance for the senior adult if the pastor asks questions about topics discussed in that area of the assessment tool (part V, spiritual component).

Timid senior adults or superficial conversations. When the caregiver visits older members who do not initiate conversation (a situation awkward for visitor and member alike) or who stick to superficial subjects, the caregiver can informally engage them in pastoral conversation by focusing on a nonthreatening area from the assessment tool, such as worship (part II, spiritual component). This subject is one they know about, and I have found that even if they have not worshipped regularly, they usually talk easily and freely about the role of worship (or its lack) in their lives. The caregiver and the aging person can explore worship patterns from childhood and youth, young adult years, mature adult years, and recent years. As this talk draws to a close, the caregiver can continue slowly and informally to guide the discussion into succeeding parts of the spiritual component.

Initial visits. This tool can be used informally if the pastor is new in the parish or has not previously visited the homebound elder. It can help to build a trust level if the visitor begins with the least threatening parts of the wholistic tool. To keep the discussion nonthreatening, one can draw these parts from throughout the tool, rather than taking them in order, as a way of getting to know the senior adult.

Subsequent visits. If the caregiver has already made several visits, some areas of the tool will already have been discussed. The caregiver can then focus on areas that have not been part of previous conversations or have not been discussed in depth. If the pastor has served the parish for many years, has visited the member many times, and fears there is nothing else to talk about, he or she will be pleased to discover that fruitful areas remain to be explored through using this assessment tool.

Thus, when the tool is used informally, those visited do not even know that it is being used. Its use, however, adds depth to subjects that senior adults raise and enables the caregiver to propose subjects for discussion when the parishioner has no agenda. In my home visits with seniors, I most often use the tool informally. I find it fascinating to guide senior adults through the spiritual as well as the other components, to analyze theological themes and patterns in their faith journeys, to assist them to draw on positive life-long learnings for continued inner strength, and to encourage them to use their learnings and strengths to deal with the challenges of aging.

Using the Tool Formally

In visits. When using the Parish Spiritual Assessment Tool formally, the pastor or other caregiver may opt to rename it to avoid the implication that its only purpose is to allow the caregiver to assess "right or wrong" responses. The name "Spiritual Journey Exercise" is congruent with the goal of assisting older people to develop an overview of their lives so that they may experience spiritual growth, comfort, and hope. Since the phrase "spiritual journey" may be part of their vocabularies and life experiences, this term may be less threatening than "spiritual assessment."

After considering which senior members would benefit from a formal use of the tool and might welcome its use, the caregiver should meet with each homebound member to define the Spiritual Journey Exercise and describe the process. The caregiver may explain the exercise in the following ways:

- The Spiritual Journey Exercise is an in-depth spiritual exercise that will help you find deeper meaning in life through reviewing how God's love was present in earlier years, is present today, and will continue to be present in the future.

- This process of spiritual growth will probably require several visits, the number to be determined by our conversations.

- I will bring a copy of the Spiritual Journey Exercise to our visits to aid the process and to take notes. I will also bring a copy for you to follow [The "Spiritual Journey Exercise for Individuals" is found in appendix A and on the accompanying CD-ROM.]. There is no need for you to do written work before our visits unless you so choose.

- Everything that you share with me will be held in strict confidence.

- You may decline to discuss any area of the exercise or discontinue the process at any time.

When the Parish Spiritual Assessment Tool is used formally, conversation follows a structured format. It is usually best to begin with the spiritual component because spirituality is the focus of ministry, and senior adults may well expect pastoral visitation to include discussions of their faith. Throughout the visits, the caregiver guides the conversation, using the format provided. In the process, both senior adults and caregivers may grow in faith.

At home alone. The "Spiritual Journey Exercise for Individuals" may be used formally by older adults who prefer to work on their spiritual growth privately through reflection and writing in a journal, by responding to the exercise questions, or by using the outline as a guide to write or record on audio- or videotape a spiritual autobiography as a gift to one's family or friends.

Guidelines for Using the Tool

The following guidelines are designed to help the pastor or other caregiver to be an empathic and inspirational guide when using the Parish Spiritual Assessment Tool either informally or formally:

1. Remember that visitation using this tool can be life-changing for senior adults.

2. When the caregiver knows those visited on a personal level, he or she is encouraged to engage in pastoral counseling as appropriate beyond the scope of this tool.

3. Frequently ask, "Do you have further insights or questions about this area of your life?" and "Would you share more about that with me?" Or simply say, "Tell me more."

4. Anticipate that senior adults may raise subjects about which they have wondered all their lives but have never discussed. Value this trust. Respond sincerely, sensitively, and expertly.

5. Remember that this process may be emotionally upsetting for senior adults. Do not shy away from discussions about the meaning of tears.

6. Do not drop a subject that parishioners raise merely because you feel uncomfortable, unless your discomfort precludes sensitive pastoral care or you are unqualified to discuss the topic. In either case, explain briefly why you are changing the subject.

7. Remember to explore constantly the meaning that the various areas have had for senior adults in the past and present, and connect this with meaning for the future.

8. Constantly offer the people you visit the assurance of God's love in Christ's ongoing presence, strength, love, hope, and peace.

9. Occasionally this tool may evoke more pain than parishioners can handle. In that case, discontinue the process and offer to explore the area of pain or make a referral to a professional therapist.

10. "Take your shoes off," for you are walking on the "holy ground" of senior adults' lives.

Whether the assessment tool is used informally or formally, no specific timetable is set for completion. For some, it may never be completed. Indeed, how *could* it ever be complete, considering the developmental nature of the faith journey?

The caregiver needs to take responsibility for time management during visits because while the visitor has a number of home visits to make in one day, homebound elders may have unlimited time and needs. When this tool is used, there will never be enough time to discuss all areas of interest. That is one reason this tool works so well. Both members and caregivers will look forward to the next visit to continue their pastoral conversation.

Taking and Using Notes

To encourage accountability, I suggest that the caregiver monitor the schedule of visits so that homebound members are visited regularly and with equal frequency (except when crises demand more frequent contact with a member). It is also wise to keep notes on the visits. I monitor my visiting schedule on graph paper, and I write notes when I return to my car after a visit. A laptop computer is helpful for keeping notes. If it is kept in the car, notes can be recorded immediately, minimizing the risk of forgetting important themes of the conversation. No more than five minutes are needed for entry. The assessment tool can be downloaded into the laptop, creating an organized format of note-taking that will also be available for review before the next home visit.

While talking about topics covered in the spiritual component, senior adults are likely to bring in subjects from other components (psychological, family, socioeconomic, medical) as well. The pastor who follows their lead will make notes in the appropriate section, so that when those topics are raised later, the caregiver will recall the previous conversation and the content of the discussion.

Reviewing notes before a follow-up visit takes me less than five minutes. Perusing notes (including the assessment and plan for the follow-up visit) affirms the importance of the previous discussion and enables follow-up conversation to be based on the earlier visit's assessment and follow-up plan. Reviewing notes also challenges the pastor to be sure to discuss important areas of faith throughout the course of visitation. Here the entire process comes together for effective pastoral care.

The information recorded must be kept confidential. Do not disclose any information from your visits to anyone. If the one you visit chooses to talk to others, that is his or her option–not yours. Do not put the information on a computer used by anyone else. Do not use the church office computer.

Do not use the personal computer in the pastor's office if the door is sometimes left unlocked and no computer password is used to protect the data. If notes are handwritten, do not leave them on a desk or in a file cabinet where anyone else may read them. Respect your members' privacy, honor their trust in you, and observe the confidentiality required by your ministry.

How to Use the Assessment and Plan Process

The assessment and plan process is essential to visitation with senior adults using the Parish Spiritual Assessment Tool. The process is the same for each component. It varies only in respect to the area of life assessed. The method is consistent. The process is illustrated in chapters 2 through 6, as ministry in each wholistic area is described. Do not be overwhelmed by the description of the process itself. In practice, the process takes no more than five minutes.

Professional objectivity. I begin part I of the process by asking myself, "How do I feel about this senior adult?" (part I, A). I hope that I am not unusual in saying that I like and love all those whom I visit. I am aware, however, of dynamics that may present challenges. For example, some of those I visit initiate conversation; some do not. Some are willing to share feelings; some are not. Some have a positive view of life; some do not. Some try to impress me. Some want to serve refreshments or feel that doing so is an obligation (their hospitality can easily lead to weight gain). Some smoke or wear perfume (which creates discomfort when I have an allergy). I try to be aware of these challenges, both before and during a visit, so that I am prepared to handle them in a professional manner.

Next I ask myself, "Does she or he have life issues similar to mine that would make it difficult for me to be objective?" (part 1, B). For example, if the senior adult needs help dealing with loneliness or depression, I need to maintain my objectivity and not think that my own strategies and skills for coping with loneliness and depression will necessarily be effective for the homebound adult. Other approaches may work better for the member. And if the older person has a view of God different from mine, I need to discuss that view objectively, not my own.

I also ask myself, "Do I have countertransference issues? Is so what, are they?" (part I, C). I need to be aware that if I relate to this person as my parent (or other relative) or friend, instead of as my parishioner or client, I may not be able to provide objective pastoral care. If I become aware that

I am viewing someone in this way, I tell myself not to act on this view. Instead, I should relate to the senior adult as a unique member who needs my objectivity.

Then I ask myself, "Does the senior adult have transference issues? If so, what are they?" (part I, D). If I am aware that the senior adult views me cognitively or emotionally as a figure from the past, such as a previous pastor or teacher, daughter or sister, I must take care not to perpetuate that tendency. I should also realize that the senior adult may subconsciously relate to me as someone in his or her past, even when I am unaware of that dynamic. An awareness that countertransference and transference may come into play ensures that we can be more effective pastoral care providers.

Senior adult's agenda. In part II of the assessment and plan process, I focus on the senior adult's agenda. I ask myself, "What does the senior adult want spiritually, psychologically, familially, socioeconomically, and medically?" The senior adult may not want anything beyond the ministry that I regularly provide. If the senior adult does want something, that desire may or may not coincide with my assessment (in part III) of what I believe she or he needs.

Pastor's or other caregiver's assessment. In part III, when my assessment of the senior adult's wholistic needs indicates that the member's current life experience is positive, I rejoice. Then I develop a follow-up plan to foster even further growth and meaning in each wholistic subject area under discussion, or (if the topic has already been covered in depth) I select a different subject from the same component, or I guide us toward exploring a different component at the next visit.

Again, the caregiver's assessment of the parishioner's wholistic needs may not be the same as that person's expressed desires in part II. For example, the senior adult may already have four lay visitors paying a call each month and want still more visits. I may not assess this want as feasible, since the majority of our homebound seniors have only one lay visitor a month.

Plan for responding to needs. When I conclude that the senior adult has an area of need, I proceed to the "Plan for Responding to the Senior Adult's Needs" (part IV). As I use the format, I ask myself, "What church resources are available to address the senior adult's needs?" (part IV, A) and "Who is available to contact the resource people?" (part IV, A, 1). After I determine the available resources and who can make the contact, I ask, "When will the contact be made?" (part IV, A, 2) and "When will the plan be implemented?" (part IV, A, 3).

Critical needs require immediate attention. For example, when a senior adult wants to "end it all" (psychological component), is seriously ill and wants to plan her funeral (spiritual component), verbally abuses the caregiver spouse (family component), has run out of money and has no food in the house (socioeconomic component), or falls many times a day and has difficulty getting up (medical component), I need to respond quickly. In some situations I may be able to delegate part of the response to available resource people (committee chairs, office manager, family members, friends of the senior adult, lay pastoral care providers, or pastoral care coordinator). Setting a date to follow up and to ensure that the plan has been carried out can be crucial so that the senior adult's ongoing needs are not neglected.

When the assessment and plan indicate that resources beyond the reach of the congregation are needed to respond adequately, I ask myself, "What community resources are available to address the senior adult's needs (for example, counseling centers and support groups, adult day care, home health nurses and aides, meals-on-wheels, chore service, low-income legal assistance, government-sponsored medical assistance, senior citizen center)?" (part IV, B), and "Who will contact the appropriate resource people?" (part IV, B, 1).

In some situations it may be empowering for the senior adult to make the contact. For example, when depressed elders decide to seek psychotherapy to address feelings of despair, it is more therapeutic for them to make the initial appointment with the therapist than for me to make the appointment on their behalf. In other situations, when senior adults are unable to make contacts with community resources and no other appropriate person is available, I will need to do it myself.

The questions "When will the contact be made?" (part IV, B, 2) and "When will the plan be implemented?" (part IV, B, 3) should be asked because some areas of need require immediate attention. The pastor or other caregiver may feel frustrated in seeking assistance from a community agency that follows slow, burdensome legal procedures. Establishing a follow-up date can be crucial to ensure that the plan has been carried out (part IV, B, 4) and that the senior adult's needs have not been overlooked.

Possible consequences. After I make an assessment and develop a plan to respond to needs, I ask myself (part V), "What are the likely consequences if I elect to do less or more than needed?" It is easy at the end of a home visit to think that I have done my pastoral duty with this senior adult for the month and go on to visits with other members or other parish responsibilities. However, there is more to geriatric ministry than keeping statistics on numbers of visits.

I have included this question as a way of raising the caregiver's awareness of the importance of accountability and responsibility in visitation. I do not imply that those who pay pastoral visits are all-powerful in members' lives. Other factors greatly affect the quality of senior adults' lives, such as their right to make unwise decisions, the role of family members, financial means, the competence of medical providers, and the laws of the state. Yet I believe that when the caregiver anticipates that a senior adult's problem could soon become too serious for the senior to handle alone, one has a professional and ethical (and sometimes legal) responsibility to assist the member immediately and appropriately. Doing less could in some situations put the aging person at greater risk of harm. On the other hand, doing more than necessary may usurp the prerogative of a senior adult who needs to feel empowered and in control. Although it is not always easy to make the distinction, the pastor or caregiver should try to determine the difference and respond appropriately. I would rather err on the side of compassion, love, and competence than to risk neglecting the senior parishioner.

As you use the Parish Spiritual Assessment Tool, I hope you will find, as I do, that you look forward to your visits. It is fulfilling to be the vehicle through which God works to bring love, meaning, and peace to senior adults.

Parish Spiritual Assessment Tool

Spiritual Component

I. Church Background

  A. How long have you been a member of our congregation?
  B. If you have been a member of other congregations, which congregations were they and what denominations? What differences did you notice?
  C. What do you most appreciate about being a member of our congregation?
  D. If other members of your family belong to a church, where are they members and what is their denomination?

II. Worship

  A. How often did you attend worship during your (1) childhood and youth, (2) young adult years, (3) mature adult years, and (4) during the past two years?
  B. If you did not attend regularly, what was your reason?
    1. Transportation limitations
    2. Weather
    3. Structural factors at the church (for example, too many steps, heavy doors, no elevator)
    4. Physical limitations
    5. Psychological or spiritual challenges (possibly including anger at the pastor, the congregation, or God)
    6. Lack of interest
    7. Other
  C. Do you listen to radio broadcasts of Sunday worship? If so, which ones, and what meaning do they have for you?
  D. Do you watch television broadcasts of religious programming? If so, which ones and how are they meaningful for you?
  E. What are some of your favorite hymns? How are they meaningful for you?
  F. In which church groups or activities were or are you active?

III. Scripture
   A. What are some of your favorite Bible passages and stories and what meaning do they have for you?
   B. What are your favorite parts of the Bible? Why are they favorites?
   C. How often do you read the Bible?
   D. Do you read devotional books or other spiritual literature? If so, which ones?

IV. Prayer
   A. What are your preferred forms of prayer?
      1. Personal free-flowing prayer
      2. Prayers during worship services
      3. Memorized bedtime prayer
      4. Music: hymns, choral, instrumental
      5. The Lord's Prayer
      6. Table grace
      7. Silent prayer
      8. Printed prayers
      9. Other
   B. For what do you pray?
   C. How often do you pray?
   D. If you struggle with prayer, would you like to talk about it?

V. Sacraments
   A. What have you been told about your baptism, or what do you remember?
   B. What does it mean to you that you are baptized?
   C. Have there been especially significant baptisms in your family or among your friends? What made them significant?
   D. What do you remember about your first communion?
   E. What does Holy Communion mean to you?
   F. How often do you like to receive Holy Communion?

VI. God
   A. How do you view God? As a God of:
      1. Love and mercy
      2. Anger and judgment
      3. Distance and hiddenness
      4. Peace and joy
      5. Promise and hope
      6. Control
      7. Other
   B. What role has God had throughout your life?
   C. Do you sometimes become angry with God? If so, when? How do you feel about being angry with God?

D. How did you serve God before you retired?
E. How do you serve God in your retirement?

VII. Jesus
A. Who is Jesus for you?

1. Friend	4. Savior
2. Comforter	5. Teacher
3. Shepherd	6. Other

B. To what extent is Jesus a source of comfort and strength for you?
C. Do you believe that God forgives your sins through Jesus' death and resurrection?
D. Do you have past or current sins that still trouble you? If so, would you like to talk about them?

VIII. Meaning
A. What were the most meaningful religious events and spiritual experiences in your childhood and youth? What meaning did they have for you?
B. What have been the most meaningful religious events and spiritual experiences in your adulthood? What meaning did they have for you?
C. Do you have a reason to get up each day? If so, what is it?
D. How has the meaning of your life changed over the years?
E. Does your faith give meaning to your life? If so, how?
F. What is your philosophy of life?
G. Do you find meaning in illness, stress, and affliction? If so, what have you found?
H. How do you cope with illness, stress, and affliction?

1. Become depressed	5. Pray for strength and comfort
2. Give up	6. Trust God
3. Shed tears	7. Seek options
4. Pray laments ("Why me?" "How long?")	8. Talk to family and friends
	9. Other

I. Have you experienced meaningful dreams, religious or nonreligious? If so, would you like to describe a dream and its meaning?
J. How do you meaningfully contribute to the well-being of others?
1. Volunteer work, such as ________________
2. Doing good deeds for others, such as ________________
3. Sharing my creative expertise with others, such as ________

IX. Death and Afterlife

A. What significant deaths have you experienced among your family and friends?
B. Have you had any near-death experiences? If so, would you describe them and the meaning they had for you?
C. Do you fear death? If so, what do you fear?
D. What do you want to do before you die?
E. Is there anything you would like to say to anyone before you die? Can you tell this person? When?
F. What is your view of the afterlife?
G. If you believe in heaven, what do you look forward to there?
H. As you look ahead to your inevitable death, what would you prefer to have in your last days?
    1. Family presence
    2. Close friends' presence
    3. Pastoral presence
    4. Be alone
    5. Holy Communion
    6. Holy Scripture
    7. Recorded music, such as ___
    8. Other responses
I. Have you planned your funeral and burial? If not, would you like help in doing so?
J. Do you have a living will? Would you like assistance in making arrangements for one?

X. Christian Decision-making

A. Does your faith help you make decisions? If so, how?
B. How often do you try to discover God's will for you when you have decisions to make?
C. What most strongly influences your decision-making?
D. What types of decisions do you allow others to help you make?
E. What types of decisions do you want to make by yourself?

XI. Peace

A. How often do you experience inner peace?
B. When do you experience inner peace?
C. If you do not experience inner peace, what hinders you from experiencing it?

XII. Faith

- A. What nurtures your faith?
  1. Worship attendance
  2. Bible reading
  3. Prayer
  4. Pastoral visitation
  5. Spiritual Journey Exercise for Individuals
  6. Holy Communion
  7. Devotional reading
  8. The sharing of my faith
  9. Religious art and music
- B. How can the pastor help nurture your faith?
- C. *[Pastor's observations of religious items]*

XIII. Religious questions

- A. Do you have religious questions that you would like to discuss?

XIV. Senior adult ministry

- A. Do you have suggestions or ideas for deepening the spiritual lives of senior adults in our congregation?
- B. Do you know other senior adults who may need home visitation or communion?

Psychological Component

I. Happiness

- A. What was the happiest time in your life? Why was it happy? Was your happiness connected to your faith? How?
- B. What makes you happy now? Why? Is the meaning of your happiness connected to your faith?
- C. What are your interests and hobbies?
- D. What are your three greatest strengths?
- E. What are your major accomplishments in life?
- F. What treasured keepsakes are most important to you? What meaning do they have for you?

II. Stress Level

- A. What is the most difficult or unhappy situation you have had to face in life? How did you cope with it?
- B. Have you been physically or verbally abused as a child or adult? If so, would you like to talk about it?

C. Are you being abused now? If so, would it be helpful to talk about it?
D. Do you feel safe at night? If not, what do you fear? What can be done to reduce your fear?
E. How do you feel in inclement weather? If you are frightened, how do you deal with your fear?
F. How much do you fear developing Alzheimer's disease?
G. Do you have questions about Alzheimer's disease? Do you need help finding the answers?
H. How often do you worry?
I. What is now causing you worry or distress?

III. Loneliness
- A. How often are you lonely?
- B. How do you deal with loneliness?
  1. Call on your relationship with God.
     - a) Pray and know God is with me.
     - b) Read my Bible and hear God speak to me.
  2. Pursue your interests.
     - a) Watch television.
     - b) Pursue hobbies.
     - c) Surf the Internet.
     - d) Read books and magazines.
     - e) Cook and eat.
     - f) Keep busy.
     - g) Listen to music.
     - h) Other.
  3. Reach out to people.
     - a) Call friends.
     - b) Call family member.
     - c) Attend senior citizen center.
     - d) Attend adult day services
     - e) Go to church events.
  4. Enjoy nature.
     - a) Watch birds.
     - b) Watch trees.
     - c) Watch clouds.
     - d) Enjoy pets.

IV. Depression
- A. Do you feel as much pleasure in life as you once did? Do the things that used to make you happy still do so? If not, how often do you feel in a low mood?
- B. How do you deal with a low mood?
  1. Healthy ways–for example:
     - a) Talk to a friend.
     - b) Talk to a pastor.
     - c) Talk to a family member.
     - g) Practice hobbies.
     - h) Exercise.
     - i) Surf the Internet.

d) Take antidepressants.
e) See a therapist.
f) Pray.
j) Enjoy pets.
k) Other.

2. Unhealthy ways–for example:
   a) Eat too much or refrain from eating.
   b) Sleep excessively.
   c) Ruminate on negative thoughts.
   d) Sit and stare.
   e) Drink alcohol to excess.

C. Have you recently experienced changes in your sleep patterns or eating habits?
D. Have you ever felt that life was not worth living? Did you receive professional help at that time? What helped you?
E. Do you feel now that life is worth living? If not:
   1. Are you feeling suicidal?
   2. Do you have a plan for ending your life?
   3. Let's talk about what is stressful in your life.
   4. [If appropriate] Let's talk about what has helped you in similar situations in the past.
   5. [If appropriate] I would like to take you [or refer you] to a professional counselor.

V. Perspective on Aging
   A. What are the best things about your age now?
   B. What do you hope for as you grow older?
   C. What is the most difficult part of growing old?
   D. What do you hope that you never have to give up?
   E. What is your secret to living a long life?
   F. What is the biggest change you have experienced in your lifetime?
   G. If you could share words of wisdom with younger people, what would you share?

VI. Support
   A. Do you have someone in whom to confide? Who? Where does she or he live? How is she or he helpful to you?
   B. Do you have close friends? Who? Where do they live? How are they helpful to you?
   C. Who are the most important people in your life now? How are they important?

Family Component

I. Childhood
- A. Where were you born and raised?
- B. What was your childhood like?
- C. By whom were you primarily raised?
- D. Did you experience major crises as a child? What were they? What meaning did they have? How did God help you through the crises?

II. Parents
- A. Are your parents still living?
- B. If so, are you their caretaker?
- C. If not, how old were you when your parents died?
- D. What were the circumstances of their deaths?
- E. How did their deaths affect you?
- F. What did you learn from them?

III. Siblings
- A. Do you have siblings? If so, how many do you have?
- B. What is your birth order? How do you think your birth order affected your early years?
- C. How many of your siblings are alive?
- D. Do they live nearby?
- E. Tell me about your relationship with your siblings.

IV. Marital Status
- A. Are you married?
  1. If so, how long have you been married?
  2. Where were you married?
  3. Have you celebrated any special anniversaries or events?
  4. How has God been a part of your marriage?
- B. If you are a widow [widower], how long ago did your spouse die?
  1. Where did your spouse die (at home or elsewhere)?
  2. What was the cause of death?
  3. What helped you work through your grief?
     - a) Family members
     - b) Friends
     - c) God
     - f) Books on grief
     - g) Support group
     - h) Hobbies

d) Congregation's ministry i) A busy routine
e) Work (including volunteer)
4. Did your spouse have Alzheimer's or some form of dementia?
5. Were you a caretaker for your spouse? If so, for how long?
6. Tell me about your spouse.
7. How have you made a new life for yourself?

C. If you are divorced, how long have you been divorced?
1. How do you feel about the divorce now?
2. How have you made a new life for yourself?

D. If you are single, what opportunities have you had as a single person that you might not have experienced if you had married?
1. What led to your decision not to marry?
2. How do you feel about not being, or not having been, married?

V. Children
A. Do you have children?
B. How many?
C. Are they all living? If not, what was [were] the circumstance of the death[s]?
D. Where do your children live?
E. What values have you attempted to pass on to your children?
F. Are your children able and willing to help you with some of your needs now?
G. Do you have grandchildren and great-grandchildren?
H. How do they bring joy to your life?

VI. Emergency contact
A. Whom should we contact for you in an emergency? What are the day-time and evening telephone numbers? Mailing address? E-mail address?

Socioeconomic Component

I. Employment
A. Have you been employed outside the home?
B. What jobs have you had both inside and outside the home?
C. How long did you work in each position?
D. What did you enjoy most about each position?
E. What did you dislike most about each position?

II. Retirement
  A. Have you retired? Partially retired?
  B. What factors led to your retirement?
  C. What has life been like since retirement?

III. Financial
  A. Are you concerned about finances?
  B. How do you get along at the end of the month when your Social Security check runs out?
  C. Do you have enough to eat?
  D. Do you participate in the Fair Share Food program?
  E. Have you assigned power of attorney to someone? If so, to whom?
  F. Do you have a will or other estate plan such as a living trust?
  G. Are you able to purchase prescribed medications?
  H. Do you have Medicare supplement insurance?
  I. *[Pastoral information: Is she or he a ward of the state?]*

IV. Time
  A. How do you spend your days and evenings? What meaning do you experience?

V. Socialization
  A. How do you socialize with others?
  B. How many times during the past week did you talk with a friend or family member?

VI. Living situation
  A. Own home
  B. Sold home to rent apartment
  C. Senior apartment without meals
  D. Senior apartment with meals
  E. Assisted-living facility
  F. Board-and-care home
  G. Nursing home
  H. Continuing care retirement community

VII. Education
  A. What is the highest educational level you have completed?

B. Where did you attend school?
C. What area of study did you enjoy most?

VIII. Societal limitation factors
A. Do these societal limitations impinge upon your life satisfaction?
1. People in authority who ignore your ability as an older adult to assess your own needs. What are some examples?
2. Gender stereotypes that dictate what people can and cannot do. What are some examples?
3. Medicare reimbursement that limits the choice of a physician to one who will exclusively accept only what Medicare will pay, thus making it difficult or impossible for you to see more expensive specialists who may be needed or desired.
4. Lack of public transportation or inability to use public transportation (in some communities, lack of public transportation) after one no longer drives.
5. Stereotypes about aging. What are some of those stereotypes?

Medical Component

I. Reasons for being homebound
A. Temporarily homebound by:
1. Illness, accident, or convalescence after hospitalization
2. Caring for invalid spouse or family member
3. Inclement weather
4. Time of day
B. Permanently homebound by:
1. Physical limitations
2. Psychological distress
3. Lack of transportation

II. Health status
A. How would you describe your health over the past year or two?
B. What health conditions affect you now?
1. Hearing impairment
2. Kidney disease
3. Heart problems
12. Visual impairment
13. Cancer
14. Stroke

4. Falls
5. Diabetes
6. Previous surgeries
7. Arthritis
8. Migraine headaches
9. Breathing problems
10. Dental problems
11. Weakness or dizziness
15. Broken hip
16. Effects of smoking
17. Problems with legs or feet
18. Osteoporosis
19. Sleep problems
20. Lack of endurance
21. Allergies
22. Addiction

C. What meaning do your health problems have for you?
D. What meaning do they have for you spiritually?
E. Have you granted someone power of attorney for health care? If so, whom? Have you discussed this arrangement with family members?
F. What home health assistance do you receive?
   1. Nursing care
   2. Assistance with bathing
   3. Housecleaning or help with other home maintenance
   4. Meals-on-wheels
   5. Assistance with laundry
   6. Medication management

III. Observations
   A. Observed physical energy level of person visited
   B. Observed cognitive function

Assessment and Plan Process

I. Professional Objectivity
   A. How do I feel about this senior adult?
   B. Does she or he have life issues that are similar to mine which would make it difficult for me to be objective?
   C. Do I have countertransference issues? If so, what are they?
   D. Does the senior adult have transference issues? If so, what are they?

II. Senior Adult's Agenda
   A. What does the senior adult want?
      1. Spiritually ____________________
      2. Psychologically ____________________

3. Familially ______________________
4. Socioeconomically ______________________
5. Medically ______________________

III. Pastor's or Other Caregiver's Assessment
   A. Spiritual
      1. Assessment ______________________
      2. Ways to foster growth ______________________
   B. Psychological
      1. Assessment ______________________
      2. Ways to foster growth ______________________
   C. Family
      1. Assessment ______________________
      2. Ways to foster growth ______________________
   D. Socioeconomic
      1. Assessment ______________________
      2. Ways to foster growth ______________________
   E. Medical
      1. Assessment ______________________
      2. Ways to foster growth ______________________

IV. Plan for Responding to the Senior Adult's Needs
   A. What church resources are available to address the senior adult's needs (for example, prayer chain, senior advisory committee, food shelf, clothing closet, Stephen Ministries, large-print Bibles, pastor)?

      ____

      1. Who is available to contact the resource people?
         a) Pastor
         b) Committee Chairperson
         c) Pastoral care coordinator
         d) Family member or friend
         e) Lay care provider
         f) Office manager
      2. When will the contact be made? ______________________
      3. When will the plan be implemented? ______________________
      4. Date on which to provide for follow-up ______________________
   B. What community resources are available to address the senior adult's needs (for example, counseling centers and support groups, adult day care, home health nurses and aides, meals-on-wheels, chore service, low-income legal assistance, government-sponsored medical assistance, senior-citizen center)?

      ____

1. Who is available to contact the resource providers?
   a) Senior adult
   b) Family or friend
   c) Pastoral coordinator
   d) Committee member
   e) Office manager
   f) Person given power of attorney
   g) Lay care provider
   h) Pastor
2. When will the contact be made? ______________
3. When will the plan be implemented? ______________
4. Date on which to provide for follow-up ______________

V. Likely Consequences if the Pastor or Other Caregiver Elects to Do Less or More than Expected or Needed:
   A. Spiritual consequences ______________
   B. Psychological consequences ______________
   C. Family consequences ______________
   D. Socioeconomic consequences ______________
   E. Medical consequences ______________

PART II

How to Use the Parish Spiritual Assessment Tool

CHAPTER 2

Exploring the Spiritual Life

Nettie: Losing the Will to Live

I always look forward to my visits with Nettie. No one I have ever known has had a stronger will to live than Nettie, so I was startled to hear her say, "I have no reason to get up in the morning anymore." I thought maybe I had not heard correctly, but when I asked again what she had said, she quietly repeated herself.

Nettie, age 81, was diagnosed with rheumatoid arthritis at age 32. Unfortunately she has had few periods of remission in the course of this chronic disease. She learned early that her condition demanded a way of life that went totally against the grain of her personality. She had to rest. Before the onset of the disease Nettie had been a vigorous and active outdoorsperson, and she had been an overachieving housekeeper. The rheumatoid arthritis eventually reduced her physical activity level to simple range-of-motion exercises, and sometimes even these were too strenuous. In the early years of her disease Nettie's husband did the housework, but after he suffered a heart attack, they hired someone to do the housecleaning, laundry, and yard work. The pain and swelling in Nettie's hands and feet, as well as the stiffness in her body, became so severe (despite the use of anti-inflammatory medications) that even the light touch of my hand giving her Holy Communion made her flinch.

After Nettie was diagnosed with rheumatoid arthritis, she continued teaching Sunday school as long as she was able. Nettie loved children but had none of her own. She also loved the Lord and loved our congregation–she was a lifelong member. She attended weekly worship and was a member of the women's group until she could no longer get in and out of a car. When both she and her husband became homebound, one of our members brought them the sermon tape and bulletin each Sunday. Nettie read one chapter in her Bible every day. Since her arthritic hands prevented her from writing her usual notes on each chapter, she began to tape-record the notes. She regularly played back the recording as words of inspiration. She especially loved the story of Jesus calming the storm on the Sea of Galilee. To her it meant that Jesus would always calm the storms in her life. Nettie "prayed without ceasing." Despite her disease, she was at peace with her God and with herself. She drew daily meaning in life from her relationship with Jesus, her constant companion and friend.

Nettie had never before even hinted at a temptation to give up on life. She had repeatedly stated that her faith was her coping mechanism for dealing with her chronic condition. Previously her attitude was upbeat. She was interested in life, including the new inventions she read about in science magazines. She inspired all who visited her with her way of dealing with life's afflictions. That is why it seemed so out of character for Nettie to say today, "I have no reason to get up in the morning anymore."

Spiritual Issues

The Parish Spiritual Assessment Tool begins with the spiritual component because spirituality is the primary focus for parish pastors and lay visitors. A relationship with God is often the foundation of senior adults' lives, providing guidance for daily living. The areas I include in the spiritual component are not an exhaustive list of spiritual issues. These are areas I have found to be important in geriatric ministry and to be directly related to the goals of the assessment tool. They assist older people "to find meaning in life from discovering how God's love and presence connect with their past, present, and future lives." Senior adults are encouraged to identify areas of inner strength and to apply them to current and future life situations.

I. Church Background

When I make an initial visit or use the Parish Spiritual Assessment Tool for the first time, I often begin with church background (part I, A). This is usually a nonthreatening area of discussion, since a relationship to our congregation is probably the reason for my visit. In some cases, senior adults join the congregation for reasons directly related to aging. For example, they may join because they can no longer drive the greater distance to a previous congregation, because they need the programs of our congregation's senior adult ministry, or because they relocate in their advanced years to a different community and congregation to be near an adult child.

When I inquire about other congregations of which they have been members (part I, B), I can sometimes discern the scope of their theological reflection and their preferred forms of worship as we compare their former congregation to ours. If they have come from another denomination, our conversation may compare denominational beliefs and practices.

When I ask senior adults what they most appreciate about our congregation (part I, C), many express positive feelings. Some, however, who have been members of our congregation for years but are only now receiving their first visit, may express unresolved spiritual distress. The senior adult may recount a negative experience from the past with a pastor, member, church program, congregational decision, or denominational doctrine. The caregiver needs to accept those feelings and respond with compassion.

It is helpful to know whether senior adults' families also belong to our congregation or to the same denomination (part I, D). When close relatives are members of the congregation, not only is this a source of comfort for the individual, but it can also allow me to develop a pastoral care plan for the entire family. When seniors are distressed that their family members are affiliated with a different denomination or faith tradition, nonjudgmental pastoral care can help them better understand the religious beliefs and practices of other family members.

If some family members have no affiliation with organized religion, sensitive pastoral care should be offered. This is not an uncommon situation. Many baby boomers raised in the church are reluctant to commit to organized religion, though they may have a vital faith system. If their parents express a sense of failure and powerlessness, the caregiver can affirm the parental decision to raise a child in the faith, discuss this tendency of baby boomers, and assure aging parents of the wide scope of God's love, which extends beyond religious affiliation.

II. Worship

While the ability to attend worship services is often taken for granted, aging members' worship experiences are often complex. Since religion is frequently a primary means of coping with life's challenges and since worship is often equated with religion, senior adults' experience of worship can be crucial for their sense of inner strength, peace, and meaning. As I ask about worship patterns in childhood and youth, young adult years, mature adult years, and recent years (part II, A), I can usually see how members' relationships with God and the congregation may have changed with the challenges of aging. Sometimes I learn just how frustrated they are with the changes.

Even seniors who are able to attend worship may need great determination and energy to get to the church and to have a positive experience there. The following challenges (part II, B) may affect attendance:

- Lack of transportation
  1. A decision not to drive or an inability to drive.
  2. Unavailability of public transportation or affordable public transportation.
  3. The congregation's inability to find volunteer drivers because of fears of personal liability.
- Weather
  1. In cold weather, a chilly sanctuary or icy streets, sidewalks, and parking lots.
  2. In warm weather, a humid atmosphere or a sanctuary with no air conditioning.
- Structural factors
  1. Numerous steps at the church entrance.
  2. An excessively steep ramp.
  3. Heavy doors.
  4. No elevator.
  5. Steps that discourage senior adults from walking up to the altar for Holy Communion.

Physical challenges also may affect senior adults' worship experience:

- Poor acoustics and unclear enunciation by pastors and worship leaders (especially troubling for the hearing-impaired).

- Poor lighting (especially unsatisfactory for the visually impaired).
- Heavy worship books (especially problematic for fragile senior adults).
- Unsecured church bulletins with loose pages and many inserts (especially disconcerting for those with arthritis).
- Small print in bulletins and hymnbooks (all but unreadable for the visually impaired).
- Too much standing during the service (especially tiring for fatigued or frail senior adults).
- Uncomfortable church pews (especially unbearable for those with back problems).

Psychological and spiritual challenges may prevent an enjoyable worship experience (or even worship attendance):

- Senior adults' feeling that they must dress well and contribute generously financially, even though they are on fixed incomes.
- The suspicion that previous years of church participation and service to the congregation are forgotten or unappreciated.
- The belief that younger, more active members devalue and neglect members of advanced years.
- The conviction that new forms of worship, programming, and church practices are not as attractive to seniors as the old traditional ways.
- The assumption that older members have fulfilled their responsibilities to the congregation through service offered in younger years.

I address these challenges actively. My goals are to enable senior adults to attend worship as long as they are capable of doing so, and to ensure that they want to attend worship, knowing that they are important and valued members of the congregation.

When homebound elders become unable to attend worship services, they may suffer spiritual crises. They may sadly believe that they will never again worship or receive Holy Communion. In such a situation, my pastoral plan includes introducing them to other worship options (such as local radio broadcasts of worship [part II, C] and cable television broadcasts of religious services [part II, D]), advising them of my plan to visit them regularly and bring Holy Communion, offering them visits from lay members who will share devotions with them, and providing worship resources from the congregation (such as daily devotional readings, religious videotapes, and audiocassette tapes of the Sunday worship services). Even when such options are available for in-home worship, many still experience spiritual distress and say, "It's just not the same" (as worshipping in church) and "It feels so different." Some elderly members will gradually adjust to the change, while others will always struggle with it.

For those who live in alternative senior housing, such as assisted living facilities and nursing homes, the worship experience also can be a challenge. If there are corporate worship services led by visiting pastors or staff chaplains, new residents may find it hard to adjust to a worship service that is not intergenerational and that is attended primarily by worshippers who use canes and walkers, sit in wheelchairs, speak at inappropriate times, and sleep through part of the service. Here again, while alert elders may be grateful for the availability of corporate worship, they may say, "It just is not the same."

Knowledge of older worshippers' favorite hymns (part II, E) can be helpful to the caregiver in developing a more complete view of their theology and in assessing pastoral care needs. A favorite hymn such as "Beautiful Savior" ("Fairest Lord Jesus") or "My Jesus, I Love Thee" may indicate that senior adults are confident of Jesus' love for them and that they deeply love Jesus. A favorite hymn such as "Amazing Grace" or "What a Friend We Have in Jesus" may indicate to some senior adults that their sins are forgiven, but to others, who do not believe that God has forgiven their sins, these hymns may stir feelings of guilt. When an older member needs to experience forgiveness, the caregiver will develop an assessment and plan that address this spiritual concern.

As I learn about senior adults' past involvement in church groups, I affirm and thank those who were active. With those who were inactive, I am available to discuss the inactivity (if they want to do so). For example, Nettie, who began teaching Sunday school at age 18 and continued teaching for 25 years, had never been thanked for her years of service. She was concerned that I, along with the current congregational leadership, might believe she had never been active, especially now that advanced rheumatoid arthritis keeps her from attending worship. Nettie's husband, who had to work on Sunday, felt guilty for his lack of church involvement. He took comfort, however, in his belief that the work Nettie did for the church was his work as well. I thanked both of them.

III. Holy Scripture

As I discuss the role of Holy Scripture with senior adults, I learn more about their theology and spiritual needs, as well as help them learn more about the Bible. Often when I ask, "What are some of your favorite Bible passages and stories?" and "What meaning do they have for you?" (part III, A), the people I visit will respond with the 23rd Psalm. While they may choose this familiar psalm because they remember few other Bible passages and this one is a common favorite, nonetheless they usually say that the psalm is meaningful because it proclaims the love of the Good Shepherd for them now and in eternity. When they cite other favorite Scripture passages, often those will include other psalms, as well as texts that proclaim the promise of salvation, such as John 14:1-7, Rom. 8:37-39, Rev. 7:9-17, Rev. 21:1-7, and Rev. 21:22- 22:5. When older people raise the subject of eternal life, I find it helpful to refer to the spiritual component, part IX ("Death and Afterlife").

Answers to the question, "How often do you read the Bible?" (part III, C) may go beyond the matter of precise frequency, although in some situations that is the extent of the response. Some parishioners emphasize the importance of their Bible reading by indicating the effort it takes. Nettie told me that she read one chapter a day, took notes on it, and when she could no longer write, tape-recorded her comments on the meaning to her of each chapter.

The pastor or other caregiver can develop a plan to assist senior adults with Bible reading. Such a plan might include:

- Offering senior adults the use of a large-print Bible or cassette tapes of the Bible from the church library.
- Offering a church library loan of Bible stories on videotape.
- Suggesting how to purchase a large-print Bible or cassette tapes of the Bible.
- Suggesting a more understandable translation of the Bible.
- Providing a daily Bible reading guide.
- Providing a list of Bible passages that proclaim aging people's divinely established value, assure them of Jesus' comfort and hope, and confidently declare the promise of eternal life.

The caregiver should be aware that some members may never have read the Bible or other spiritual literature (part III, D) because of a lack of reading ability, fear that the Bible would be too difficult to understand, unavailability of a Bible, or lack of encouragement to read it. When one makes this assessment and develops a follow-up plan, this part of the spiritual component can offer the older adult a life-changing opportunity for spiritual growth.

IV. Prayer

While some senior adults have an active prayer life, others struggle with prayer and are unsure how to pray. Those who are comfortable with prayer will easily discuss their preferred forms of prayer (part IV, A). Senior adults for whom prayer is difficult may feel relieved to learn that there are a variety of prayer forms and that all forms are acceptable to God. With older parishioners who continue to struggle with prayer (and may feel guilty about it), I frequently refer to Rom. 8:26-27, in which Paul states that the Holy Spirit searches hearts and intercedes for "the saints" before God. This passage almost always brings a sense of relief to those who hear it. My assessment and plan frequently include suggesting that senior adults experiment until the next visit with a new form of prayer, such as one of those included in the spiritual component. I record this suggestion in my notes so that at our next visit I remember to ask how it went.

When senior adults feel comfortable sharing with me that for which they pray (part IV, B) and how often they pray (part IV, C), I receive their response with honor, respect, and an invitation to discuss it. For example, when Nettie states that her favorite prayer (which she prays morning, noon, and night) is "Jesus help me," I ask about areas of her life in which she needs help. Because Jesus is important in her life, I also initiate a conversation about Jesus. As I do so, I refer to another area of the spiritual component, part VII ("Jesus"), which provides a wonderful guide for our discussion.

When Nettie says that she prays for medical needs, I may bring parts of the medical component into our discussion to help me assess whether Nettie's medical situation can be improved. If Nettie tells me that she prays not to fall when she goes to the bathroom during the night, I ask whether that has happened. If she has fallen, I help her to determine the cause of the fall. I may suggest that she eliminate scatter rugs, use a cane or walker, wear shoes or slippers, leave a light on at night, and get an emergency-alert device to wear around her neck so that she can receive immediate assistance if she falls. The follow-up plan can include ways to put these suggestions into action. Here again, as spiritual and medical needs intersect, the wholistic nature of the Parish Spiritual Assessment Tool is evident.

V. Sacraments

Baptism. The discussion of sacraments begins with baptism. Through this discussion I affirmanging persons' value as loved children of God and remind senior adults that God's love remains constant regardless of limitations imposed by the aging process. Age-related challenges to body, mind, and spirit may lead older men and women to question their value to the world and to those around them. They may say, as Nettie said, "I have no reason to get up in the morning anymore." Such comments open the door for the caregiver to focus on their "being" and to discourage them from correlating their value with their productivity in society.

At such a point, the caregiver may help senior adults discover new meaning in life by referring again to another part of the spiritual component. Part VIII ("Meaning") can be of help here. As theologian Paul Tillich wrote, "[The person's] being includes [her or] his relations to meanings."[1] When older members realize that through their baptism, they are valuable to God for who they are (that is to say, their being) apart from their productivity, they will begin to base the meaning of their lives on God's unconditional love.

Discussions of older persons' own baptisms can take many forms (part V). While some aging people were told very little about their baptisms, others have fascinating stories to share. Moreover, when people tell stories about family baptisms, the caregiver should be alert for unresolved feelings from the past or for a spiritual dilemma.

Holy Communion. The discussion of Holy Communion takes place most naturally when the pastor brings communion to the homebound persons' homes. Many people in their later years will be able to remember their first communion and will share stories about confirmation instruction, the name of the pastor who confirmed and first served communion to them, and details of the first communion day (part V, D).

A natural progression is to ask what Holy Communion means to them (part V, E). Often instead of responding directly, elderly men and women begin by telling me what it is like to receive Holy Communion at home. Some seniors may not have previously known that communion can be brought to the home; thus, they express gratitude that they can continue to receive communion. Others may say they miss receiving communion with other members in the church sanctuary. In such a situation the assessment and plan may include inviting family members to join us for home communion next time; or, if that is not possible, inviting friends or lay visitors from the congregation to join us for communion (with the homebound senior's permission, of course). Occasionally older people may say that they prefer receiving communion at home because it seems more personal than in the church, since in the home usually only the senior adult, the pastor, and God are present.

In speaking of the theological meaning of Holy Communion, senior adults often refer to feelings of gratitude for Jesus' journey to the cross, forgiveness of sins, God's love, God's strength for daily life, and Jesus' promise of salvation. While some will be able to expound on their responses, others will not.

It is important for pastors and other caregivers to ask those whom they visit how often they like to receive Holy Communion (part V, F) and to update records with these preferences.

Other Sacraments. For pastors and other caregivers of denominations that recognize more than two sacraments, the discussion of sacraments will continue in a similar manner.

VI. God

It is possible for people to participate in religious ritual and yet not explore their thoughts or feelings about God (part VI, A, B, C). This can be especially true for senior adults who have been taught to discount their feelings and never to question God's ways. Exploring one's relationship with God is important for aging men and women who suffer from multiple challenges to body, mind, or spirit. They may need permission to express negative feelings about God.

Discussing with retirees the ways they have served God over the years (part VI, D) allows them to put a theological interpretation on their lives. That in turn may help them find renewed meaning in life. Talking about how they served God in previous years can spark ideas for how they can continue to serve God in retirement (part VI, F).

VII. Jesus

Almost always a discussion about the role of Jesus in senior adults' lives (part VII, A, B) turns to the comfort and assurance that Jesus provides. When seniors say that Jesus is their Friend, Comforter, Shepherd, Savior, Teacher, or a combination of these, they know what it means to live "in Christ." Through Jesus, they experience God's goodness and strength as they face the challenges of aging. When senior adults have a close relationship with Jesus, the most helpful follow-up plan is often to continue to talk about Jesus with them, because as one older member told me, "Most people won't talk about Jesus. I like it when you do."

While talking about Jesus, it is important to ask, "Do you believe that God forgives your sins?" (part VIII, C). If the parishioner hesitates to answer the question or says, "I don't know," gently ask follow-up questions: "Do you have past or current sins that still trouble you?" and "Would you like to talk about them?" (part VII, D). At the end of a conversation in which someone talks about troubling sins, I may ask if he or she would like to engage in an informal process of individual confession and absolution. When we do so, my plan for the follow-up visit includes a review of this pastoral conversation and an inquiry about how the person felt about the conversation. The discussion about forgiveness and absolution may need to continue, because realization of forgiveness is sometimes a process rather than an immediate occurrence.

VIII. Meaning

Part VIII focuses on the following goal of the Parish Spiritual Assessment Tool: "To assist the member to find meaning in life by discovering how God's love and presence connect with her or his past, present, and future life." In these discussions, the caregiver assists aging adults to live the later years of life in a spiritually meaningful way, confident that the God who was present for them in the past will continue to be with them now and in the future, and for eternity. Living with this assurance, they will have inner peace. The discussion about meaning in life will probably need to stretch over a number of visits, proceeding at the elder's pace and according to his or her agenda.

As I ask senior adults about the most significant religious events and spiritual experiences of childhood and adulthood (part VIII, A, B), I respond to each event or experience with the question, "What did that mean for you?" I also help them to identify how God's love was present, assist them in discerning their areas of inner strength in the experiences, and encourage them to reflect on how these events affected them in later years. In my assessment and plan, I make notes about these insights so that when these aging people are faced with future crises, I can remind them that God will continue to give them strength to endure each crisis, just as in the past.

After people in their later years have articulated meaningful life experiences and inner strengths, I may ask, "Do you have a reason to get up each day? If so, what is it?" (part VIII, C). Nettie's reason had been the same for years. Her reason was her relationship with Jesus, her constant friend. But as we saw in the opening story, one day she no longer had a reason to get up. While caregivers who maintain a hectic daily schedule may find it difficult to understand and address the dynamic of not having a reason to get up, too many senior adults do not have a reason to get up each day.

I encourage pastors and other caregivers not to slight this question and not to project their own reasons for getting up each morning onto retired people. Instead, listen carefully to their responses, and if you hear laments or expressions of depression, respond with empathy and offer to explore options. The caregiver's approach may include giving them permission to lament, inviting them to talk about their feelings, asking what may have changed in their lives, referring to suggestions about finding meaning in life (in this part of the spiritual component), or suggesting that they engage in the Spiritual Journey Exercise for Individuals (appendix A).

The intent of the next three questions ("How has the meaning of your life changed over the years?," "Does your faith give meaning to your life? If so, how?" and "What is your philosophy of life?" [part VIII, D, E, F]) is not to place expectations for a grandiose discourse upon the people one visits, but rather to encourage them to reflect on meaning in their lives, even if they can discern that meaning only in retrospect. Again I help them to connect important past experiences with their present lives, and to project the meaning into their future. When they share their philosophies of life, their words may offer wisdom from which caregivers can also grow. Some philosophies that aging people have expressed include these:

"Trust in the Lord and the Lord will take care of you."
"Don't give up."

"Be optimistic and on top of things."
"Don't let things bother you too much."
"Do something even if you don't feel like it."
"Laugh every day."
"Be friendly."
"There is good in everyone."

Keep notes about these conversations, because as aging people come to distressing (and perhaps meaningless) times in life, the caregiver can remind them of their philosophies expressed earlier and remind them that what provided meaning in the past may apply to their current situation.

The next two questions ("Do you find meaning in illness, stress, or affliction? If so, what is it?" and "How do you cope with illness, stress, or affliction?" [part VIII, G, H]) are related to age-old mysteries of suffering: "Why do people suffer?" "Why do I suffer?" My intent is not to summarize the many books on the subject of suffering but rather to address this concern of aging senior adults. The wise pastor or other caregiver refrains from imposing a personal view of suffering on senior parishioners. The caregiver can suggest ways of dealing with suffering (part VIII, H), such as shedding tears, uttering prayers of lament, offering up prayers for strength and comfort, trusting in God, and actively solving problems. These suggestions can be incorporated into the assessment and plan.

Even after the caregiver discusses coping strategies with senior adults who suffer, aging people may still be unable or unwilling to talk about the nature of their suffering. Instead they may ask, "Pastor, why doesn't God let me die so that I can be removed from my suffering?" Or they may suggest that life is meaningless, saying, "Pastor, I just want to die because I don't have anything to live for." While the latter remark may be a continual lament for one elderly person, it may be a statement of suicidal ideation for another. When the aging parishioner expresses suicidal feelings, the pastor can turn to part IV ("Depression") of the psychological component for guidance. An immediate assessment and plan may be needed. If the pastor or other caregiver is uncertain about the assessment, it is imperative to err on the side of caution, as well as to provide ongoing pastoral care while the despondent senior traverses this dark night of the soul.

The question "Have you experienced meaningful dreams, religious or non-religious?"(part VIII, I) affirms the meaningful role that dreams can play in senior adults' lives. It gives aging people permission to discuss their dreams.

Such discussions are especially important when the dreams are troubling. While dreams offer pastoral care opportunities, the pastor or other caregiver should remember that the only person who can interpret a dream is the dreamer.

Because peoples' lives are usually meaningfully enriched by helping other people, numerous suggestions are provided in part VIII (section J) for how senior adults can contribute to the well-being of other persons. For older men and women who are already engaged in such activities, a discussion with the caregiver about the meaning of the activities may help aging persons to discover additional life satisfaction. Senior adults who are not helping other people but would like to do so can usually find at least one suggestion from the list that they would like to try.

IX. Death and Afterlife

The discussion of death and afterlife is an indispensable area of the Parish Spiritual Assessment Tool. It should be the goal of every parish pastor to proclaim the assurance of God's eternal love in Jesus Christ so that senior adults can reflect on their deaths with a sense of confidence and peace.

The prospect of their inevitable death is a common concern of aging people. Some may experience anticipatory death as they wonder whether they will be forgotten nonpersons as they begin to suffer cognitive loss, as they ponder the diminution of appearance, performance, and physical health that precede biological death, and as they may become unable to visit with friends and relatives. Senior adults in these situations may welcome a conversation with the pastor about death and afterlife.

When I ask, "What significant deaths have you experienced among your family and friends?" (part IX, A), I glimpse the depths of grief that some senior adults have suffered, as well as its implications for other areas of their lives, such as socioeconomic well-being and psychological support. While writing notes about the deaths of family members, I also record remarks about coping skills so that in future times of loss, I can encourage seniors to use their proven inner resources for coping with grief.

Senior adults may hesitate to share near-death experiences (part IX, B) with anyone because they fear no one will believe them. Near-death experiences can be powerful and life-changing. They take many forms.

Sam, a farmer, still feels awe about one close call. "I was helping my son on the farm, and I was working with the corn picker," he remembered. "My arm got caught in it, and it bled something terrible. I passed out, and if my son hadn't arrived when he did, the doctor said I would have died."

Josephine's tendency each winter to develop serious bronchitis escalated into pneumonia, and she was hospitalized. She slipped into a coma and was placed on a ventilator. Afterward she said, "When I was in the coma, I saw the green pastures of heaven. Heaven was beautiful."

Peter and Sarah always found it a major struggle to prepare meals. Peter said to me after a fire in their kitchen, "Pastor, Sarah was surrounded by flames. Both of us saw the angels who came and surrounded her and led her safely out of the fire."

After Catherine came out of a coma following major surgery, she said, "Pastor, I saw the tunnel, and Jesus was at the end of the tunnel. When I was almost to the light at the end of the tunnel where Jesus stood, he put up his hand and said, 'You have to go back. It's not yet your time.' I didn't want to come back."

Pastors or other caregivers with whom such near-death experiences are shared need to "take off one's shoes," for they are walking on the holy ground of senior adults' lives.

The assessment and plan developed in response to these near-death stories should include a discussion with senior adults about the meaning of their experiences.

Sam said he was grateful to be alive and that now every Sunday he attends church, where he thanks God for his life.

For Josephine, the 23rd Psalm had "come to life" for her.

Peter and Sarah believed that God was telling them to move into an assisted living building where meals would be prepared for them.

Catherine became certain that Jesus had a place reserved for her in heaven.

While some people in their later years are at peace with the thought of death, others fear death (part IX, C). Often those who fear death are more afraid of the dying process than of death itself and may have existential or spiritual reasons for their fears. They may fear losing their only known world when they cross into a world about which they know little. They may voice concerns about family members left behind, fearing the effect of their death on loved ones. Arvilla sadly told me, "I'm weaning my son away from me. I'm telling him not to come and see me every day anymore. I don't like to do it, but maybe if I do, he will not miss me as much when I die." Senior adults may fear divine retribution for their sins. They may grieve over their failure to complete lifetime goals. The caregiver's assessment and plan should address these fears in a manner that will bring inner peace to senior adults.

To encourage self-reflection, I ask,"What do you want to do before you die?" (part IX, D) and "Is there anything you would like to say to anyone before you die?" (part IX, E). Some elderly people may respond, "I don't have anything further I want to do, and I've said everything I need to say." Others may not previously have thought about these questions, may now think of something they would like to say to a loved one, and may need support from me to develop the courage to follow through. The latter question is also one which I rephrase, asking adult sons and daughters, "Is there anything you would like to say to your parents before they die?" The assessment and plan should remind the caregiver to ask at the next visit whether follow-through has occurred.

Asking "What is your view of the afterlife?" (part IX, F) can lead senior adults to disclose whether they believe they will experience salvation or damnation. When they question their salvation and wish to discuss it, the caregiver should develop a plan and follow up with it. The caregiver and the parishioner may wish to follow this topic of conversation for a number of visits. Keeping good notes will assist the caregiver to follow up on previous conversations and to include new insights.

Senior adults who believe in heaven and tell what they look forward to in the afterlife (part IX, G) may express a variety of hopes and dreams. Many hope to experience relief from physical and psychological pain, to be rewarded for the sacrifices they made on earth, to recover the energy level of their younger years, to understand everything perfectly (including why there is suffering in the world), to see the God whom they have worshipped and served, to be met by Jesus who died and rose for them, and to experience divine peace. The assessment and plan will include the caregiver's availability for more conversations about their expectations of heaven. The caregiver may also provide Bible readings about heaven.

After asking, "As you look ahead to your inevitable death, which of the following would you prefer in your last days (family presence, close friends' presence, pastoral presence, being alone, Holy Communion, Holy Scripture, recorded music, other)?" (part IX, H), I document members' preferences well. When elderly members are near death, I refer to their records and follow through carefully to provide the kind of pastoral care they previously requested. They may wish to receive Holy Communion, even if it only touches their lips.

It is a natural progression after such a conversation to ask older parishioners whether they have planned their funeral and burial (part IX, I). Those who have not made funeral plans may welcome the opportunity to do so. For those who have done so, the plans may be on record at a funeral home, stuck in a Bible, or stashed in any one of several locations. Unless a relative or friend will be available at the time of death to provide the funeral plans, it is important that the pastor knows where the plans are kept or be informed of the plans. It is helpful to have a file at the church for funerals planned in advance. When aging people tell the pastor that they want to plan their funerals, it may be well to schedule another visit solely for that purpose so that they can give their plans prayerful thought and perhaps invite family members to be present for the visit. Senior adults also may ask for help with writing their obituaries, especially if family relationships are complex.

The question "Do you have a living will?" (part IX, J) can lead to an educational conversation. The pastor or other caregiver may need to explain what a living will is and answer practical or theological questions about options for sustaining or discontinuing life supports. If senior adults have living wills but have not shared them with their families, physicians, or attorneys, the caregiver can encourage them to do so.

X. Christian Decision-making

Aging adults often have decisions to make that relate to each component of the Parish Spiritual Assessment Tool.

- Spiritual decisions may include: "Am I at that point in my life when I need to ask the pastor to bring me communion at home?" "Is it really OK to be angry at God because of all the negative changes in my life?"
- Psychological decisions may be based on questions such as: "What can I do when I am afraid at night and I'm all alone?" and "How can I handle my depression?"
- Family-related decisions may include: "If I tell my children how difficult it is to live alone, will they help me to stay in my home or will they put me in a nursing home?" "How do I tell my husband that I need to sleep in a separate bedroom now because his movements and sounds during the night scare me and keep me awake?"

- Socioeconomic decisions may include: "How can I get more contact with people now that I'm nearly confined to home?" "How can I afford the expensive medication the doctor just prescribed when I'm on a fixed income?"
- Medical decisions may include: "How much longer can I take care of my invalid spouse at home?" "Do I want to go through a series of chemotherapy treatments with unpleasant side effects and trips to the doctor? Or do I want to let cancer take its course in my body?"

Some senior adults have always had trouble making decisions. For others, the person whom they always trusted for help with decision-making may have died. Still others may have a history of always second-guessing decisions. Some may worry about making the wrong decision, even when there is no right or wrong answer.

Through a series of questions, "Christian Decision-making" encourages senior adults to make decisions based on their faith systems (part X, A, B). Senior adults may wish to explore more than just the process of making a decision. They may ask the caregiver for help with a current decision. Toward the end of a visit, if the caregiver thinks there may be just enough time to go quickly through what "appears" to be a relatively short part of the spiritual component, he or she should be advised that this topic may require more time than anticipated.

XI. Peace

Inner peace is something for which many senior adults pray. This is one reason the Aaronic benediction is so meaningful for senior adults ("The LORD bless you and keep you; the LORD make his face to shine upon you, and be gracious to you; the LORD lift up his countenance upon you, and give you peace" [Num. 6:24-26]).

I frequently combine the questions, "How often do you experience inner peace?" (part XI, A) and "When do you experience inner peace?" (part XI, B). However, when senior adults say that they only infrequently experience inner peace, I immediately proceed to the next question, "What might hinder or prevent you from experiencing inner peace?" (part XI, C). As a way of helping such a senior adult to experience inner peace, I may say, "Clara, some of our senior adults experience inner peace when they pray and share their specific needs with God. Other members experience inner peace when they are with their family or friends, or when they think about the wonderful times they've had with family or friends. Still others experience inner peace when they are alone as they remember that Jesus is always with them. Do you think any of these suggestions would help you?"

If they raise a significant concern, it may need to become part of the assessment and plan in which other component areas of the assessment tool are utilized. For example, Emelia said, "I'm afraid at night of the crime in my neighborhood." Charles said, "I don't experience peace because my knee is in constant pain and I don't know what to do about it." Olaf said, "No, I'm not at peace, because I constantly wonder if I should move into a nursing home."

XII. Faith

Just as they long for inner peace, many older members seek also to grow in faith. As I ask what nurtures their faith, I often suggest ways to grow in faith based on suggestions provided in the spiritual component (part XII, A), such as Bible reading, praying, and devotional reading. As I suggest using spiritual exercises to help aging people grow in faith, I recommend the Spiritual Journey Exercise for Individuals (appendix A) and explain that we can journey through the exercise together during our visits or they can use it by themselves at home. When I ask if they have ideas for how I can nurture their faith (part XII, B), they usually say, "Just keep doing what you are already doing."

As I glance around the room where we visit (part XII, C), I look for clues to what might nurture the senior adult's faith. For example, I once mentioned to Hilda that the number of devotional books I saw on her table suggested that devotional literature must be meaningful to her. She surprised me with her vigorous response: "It sure is! I read our congregation's devotional book in the morning, my Bible at noon, and a devotional book for women before I go to bed." As we talked more about reading the Bible, Hilda began to ask me questions about the Bible that she had previously never had the courage to ask anyone: "What do I do when I come to unusual names that I cannot pronounce?" "How can I remember where I read something in the Bible?" "What should I do when I come to a passage I don't understand?" We discussed her questions, and at the conclusion of the visit I wrote her questions in my records. During our follow-up visit, I asked what she thought of my Bible reading suggestions. Hilda replied, “It’s easier to understand the Bible now, and I can read it faster and learn more.” This is growth in faith.

XIII. Religious Questions

I always try to remember to ask at each visit, “Do you have any religious questions that you would like to discuss?” (part XIII, A). If I do not specify “religious” questions, I am asked all types of questions, such as, “Can you fix the freezer in my basement?” As a trust relationship develops with the caregiver, senior adults who may have wondered about a spiritual concern for years may decide that it is safe now to ask about it.

The religious questions asked by those I visit cover a wide range of subjects: “Where did God come from?” “How does the Trinity work?” “What is the Holy Spirit?” “Does someone have to be baptized to go to heaven?” “How often do you have to confess the same sin?” “Why are some people cremated instead of buried?” “Do you believe in angels?” “What do you think of near-death experiences?” “What is the unforgivable sin?” “Why did Jesus tell his disciples not to tell anyone?” “Do we believe in predestination?” “What does it mean to be born again?”

In the course of discussion, I also seek to discern possible agendas behind the questions. Eva, who asks, “Where did God come from?” may have so many problems that she wonders if God is still present in her life. Bill, who asks, “Does someone have to be baptized to go to heaven?” may be worried about the salvation of a grandchild who has not been baptized.

As senior adults are invited to raise questions, they will ask more and more questions because the caregiver responds with pastoral care for their concerns. Notation of these questions ensures that the caregiver can remember to ask during the next visit whether the questioner would like to discuss the subject further.

XIV. Senior Adult Ministry

Periodically I ask, “Do you have suggestions or ideas for deepening the spiritual lives of senior adults in our congregation?” (part XIV, A). The most effective senior adult ministry program is built on the needs and suggestions of seniors themselves, including homebound members. An assessment and plan is needed for each suggestion.

I often ask, "Do you know of other senior adults who may need home visitation and communion?" (part XIV, B). Homebound senior adults often have a telephone support network among themselves and will know whose situations have changed. They may also know that a specific person will not call the church to request a visit. Since I regularly ask for referrals, some senior adults on my home visitation list have formed the habit of notifying me when another homebound senior needs a visit. I thank my informant for the referral and follow up as soon as possible.

Helping Nettie to Regain Spiritual Hope

As I visited with Nettie alone, I invited her to talk about what was different now, compared with times in her life when she had a reason to get up in the morning because Jesus, her friend, gave her life meaning. What was different, Nettie said, was her vision. Previously she began her day by reading the Bible. She also read Holy Scripture periodically throughout the day and evening. When she read stories of Jesus in the gospels she felt close to her Lord. For Nettie, Bible reading was also a way to pass time. Now that she cannot see to read her Bible, she feels as though she has lost her relationship with Jesus–thus, her spiritual depression.

Assessment and Plan

Part I. Professional Objectivity.

A. How do I feel about Nettie? I admire Nettie and love her as a child of God. Today I am concerned about her because for the first time in our four-year relationship she says she has lost her will to live.

B. Does Nettie have life issues similar to mine that would make it difficult for me to be objective? Perhaps. I have had arthroscopic knee surgery, which has made it necessary for me to limit the duration of some exercises I enjoy. Sometimes I wonder if I will become handicapped as I age.

C. Do I have countertransference issues? Perhaps. I have learned a great deal from Nettie about using one's faith to cope with the adversities of life. I need to remind myself to view her as a member who needs my expertise.

D. Does Nettie have transference issues? None that I can identify, unless she sees in me all the other pastors who have served her.

Part II. Senior Adult's Agenda

A. What does Nettie want?
   1. Spiritually: Nettie wants to know that Jesus is still her friend.
   2. Psychologically: Nettie wants to get over her depression.
   3. Familially: Nettie does not want to burden her husband with her problem. He has no expertise in treating spiritual depression, and he has his own medical concerns.
   4. Socioeconomically: Nettie expressed no wants or needs.
   5. Medically: Nettie wants to be able to see better.

Part III. Pastor or Other Caregiver's Assessment

A. Spiritual
   1. Assessment: Nettie is spiritually depressed.
   2. Ways to foster growth: Read aloud with Nettie her favorite Bible passage about Jesus calming the storm on the Sea of Galilee. Remind her how God has previously given her strength to cope with difficult times. Encourage her to use these inner resources now.

B. Psychological
   1. Assessment: Nettie's depression is partly due to medical reasons.
   2. Ways to foster growth: Discuss how she deals with depression.

C. Family
   1. Assessment: Nettie does not want to burden her husband with her spiritual depression.
   2. Way to foster growth: Assure Nettie and her husband that I will help them obtain medical help.

D. Socioeconomic
   1. Assessment: Nettie expressed no needs.
   2. Way to foster growth: I may refer to part V (Socialization) of the socioeconomic component and find a church volunteer to visit them.

E. Medical
   1. Assessment: Nettie's vision should be checked.
   2. Way to foster growth: Assist Nettie to make an appointment with an ophthalmologist. Arrange for transportation and a companion to go with her.

Part IV. Plan for Responding to the Senior Adult's Needs
   A. What church resources are available to address Nettie's needs? The pastor (me), the Stephen minister, and the church secretary.
      1. Who is available to contact the Stephen minister? I will do this to ensure confidentiality.
      2. When will contact be made with the Stephen minister? Immediately. I will request that Nettie and her husband be matched with a visitor for ongoing visits, as well as with someone to accompany her to her ophthalmology appointment.
      3. When will the plan be carried out? Today. I will immediately call the Stephen Ministries coordinator and Nettie's preferred ophthalmologist.
      4. Date on which to provide for follow-up. I will write her eye appointment in my appointment book, and I will schedule my follow-up visit with her as soon as possible afterward, depending on her schedule.
   B. What community resources are available to address Nettie's needs? The senior citizen center has a van with a hydraulic lift for wheel chairs.
      1. Who is available to contact the resources? The church secretary can call the senior citizen center and arrange transportation for Nettie and her Stephen Ministries companion.
      2. When will the contact be made? Today.
      3. When will the plan be implemented? On the day of the eye appointment.
      4. Date to provide for follow-up? Tomorrow. Ask the church secretary if the arrangements were made.

Part V. Likely Consequences if the Pastor or Other Caregiver Elects to Do Less or More than Expected or Needed.
   A. Spiritual consequences: If I do not follow through with Nettie, her relationship with God may be adversely affected.

B. Psychological consequences: If I do not follow through, Nettie may remain spiritually depressed. Her husband may also become depressed.
C. Family consequences: If I do not follow through, Nettie's positive relationship with her husband may be adversely affected.
D. Socioeconomic consequences: If I do not follow through (as appropriate) in addressing Nettie's need to socialize, she may become even more isolated than now.
E. Medical consequences: If I do not follow through, Nettie will not receive an eye evaluation and she will never know whether her vision can be improved.

Nettie was fortunate that her vision had not greatly deteriorated. Before her eye appointment, I brought her from the church library a large-print New Testament, which she was able to read. (The large-print Bible was too heavy for her to hold.) Nettie was told by the ophthalmologist that she had an early-stage cataract. In about two months it could be removed. Both Nettie and her husband were relieved at the positive prognosis. The ophthalmologist anticipated that Nettie would see well after the cataract was removed and she was fitted with new corrective lenses. Meanwhile she continued to read the large-print New Testament until she could no longer see the print. The Stephen minister then made a point of reading to Nettie her favorite gospel stories about Jesus. I also provided cassette tapes of the gospels from the church library. Despite her temporarily deteriorating vision, Nettie's spiritual depression lifted. Once again she knew that Jesus was her friend–and so was her church family.

CHAPTER 3

Psychological Aspects of Aging

The Smiths: Losing Control and Happiness

Marcella and Spencer Smith had been married for 55 years. As a well-loved history professor at a small four-year college, Spencer had risen in rank to serve as head of his department for the 12 years preceding his retirement. Marcella had put her liberal arts background to work by starting her own travel agency. When she retired, her 12 employees put together the vacation of a lifetime, a safari in Tanzania, as a retirement gift for Marcella and Spencer. Life had been happy for this successful couple. They were well educated, well traveled, and greatly admired by their colleagues and friends.

The Smiths did not take their happy life for granted. They counted their blessings, sharing devotions every morning and praying together every evening. Always they offered a special prayer of thanks for their only child, Susan, their pride and joy. For Susan, success had meant a life of public service as a language translator for the government. She now lived in Israel.

One day their lives changed suddenly. Spencer suffered a debilitating stroke. After his brief hospitalization, Marcella brought him home, and their normally calm existence changed to one of stress, anger, and depression. They felt as if their lives had gone out of control. The effects of the stroke consumed their waking and sleeping hours.

Spencer needed Marcella's help to transfer in and out of his wheelchair, use the bathroom, dress, and deal with his changing emotions. She stopped attending garden-club and church circle meetings–both previous "high points" of her retirement. Because she was the primary caregiver and Spencer was now an invalid, she also had become homebound. It was not long before Marcella felt isolated, lonely, and depressed.

Spencer's challenge was to accept being the recipient of almost total care. Using his one "good" arm, he could feed himself and (if he was careful) hold a book and turn its pages. Otherwise Spencer's physical abilities were limited. He was embarrassed that he needed so much assistance from Marcella and that he sometimes cried for what he thought was no reason at all. As time went by, Spencer became more frustrated and angry, until he started to take out his feelings on his wife. At times he yelled at her–something he had never done before. Occasionally he threw his book or dinner plate (with food on it) on the floor. He was confused by his new behavior, and he did not know how to deal with his new emotions.

When the pastor came to bring communion (another new experience for both Marcella and Spencer) and asked, "How are the two of you doing?" they could do no less than blurt out the whole story. After that, one of them said, "Pastor, we don't know what to do. We need help. What should we do?"

Psychological Issues

Although I include a psychological component in the Parish Spiritual Assessment Tool, the psychological concerns of senior adults are not my primary focus, nor do I function as a psychologist or psychiatrist during visits. I include this component because psychological issues often affect the well-being of senior adults. If a psychological issue tends to become the primary focus, I attempt to refer the senior to a professional therapist. If he or she resists such a referral, I make a referral to a primary-care physician.

The areas included in the psychological component are not intended to be all-inclusive. Rather, they are areas I have found to affect senior adults' happiness, their ability to experience meaning in life, and their perception of the aging process. My approach varies. Sometimes I weave parts of the psychological component into a visit that follows primarily the format of the spiritual component, because that seems to be less threatening to the aging person. At other times I focus exclusively on the psychological component. Sometimes I combine the two approaches. When I do this, however, I enter the notes from the visit into the separate components. This enables me to be more focused and efficient as I review my notes before the next visit. I base my approach on the needs and agenda of the senior adult.

I. Happiness

Since many senior adults, especially the homebound, face challenges that can disturb their psychological outlook, this component begins by focusing on positive life experiences. As I begin with the topic of happiness, my intent is not to minimize senior adults' struggles but rather to affirm that they are people of worth and goodness created in God's image, and that they have experienced some degree of God's goodness in past years. Sometimes when aging people confront problems, they tend to forget the positive experiences of the past, the inner strength God has given them to meet life's challenges, and the companions whom God has brought into their lives to encourage and support them.

This was the case for the Smiths. Although they had enjoyed much happiness during their employment and early retirement years, they forgot about God's goodness as they were faced with adjusting to the limitations imposed by Spencer's stroke. After they began to receive home health services, which helped them feel better about their situation, I encouraged them to recall that just as they had previously been blessed with positive experiences, God-given strength, and supportive friendships, the same would be true now. I assured them that God would continue to be present for them, and so would I.

Senior adults may answer the question, "What was the happiest time in your life?" (part I, A) in a variety of ways. Doris said, "The day I saw my adopted infant great-granddaughter, who had previously lived in poverty in a third-world country, was my happiest day." Curtis responded, "I was the happiest when I took a ride in a hot-air balloon." Constance firmly declared, "I was the happiest when my children graduated from school, were out on their own, and could take care of themselves, because then I could do things I like to do."

The caregiver can encourage senior adults to explore further by asking, "Why was this the happiest time in your life?" Doris went on to say, "This [adoption] made me happy because my granddaughter and her husband gave my great-granddaughter an opportunity in life she would never have had otherwise." Curtis continued, "I was happy because when I took that hot-air balloon ride I felt free from all the pressure and stress in my life." Constance said, "I was happy because after my children were out on their own, I took a short course and became a certified nursing assistant in a nursing home. I had always wanted to work in a nursing home because I love old people."

The meaning of these happy experiences can be linked to senior adults' faith by asking, "Was this meaning related to your faith in any way?" "Oh yes," Doris emphatically replied. "One of my favorite Scripture passages has always been where Jesus tells us to feed the hungry. And I know that my new great-granddaughter would have been hungry all her life in that poor country, if she had survived at all." Curtis said, "I think it was God's way of telling me that God wants me to be happy." Constance replied, "I always wanted to work in a nursing home because the Bible tells us to respect our elders and take care of widows and orphans. Old people have always been important to me–and now I'm one!"

In responding to the question, "What makes you happy now?" (part I, B), senior adults may refer to a variety of factors. Their families may be a source of satisfaction as adult children regularly telephone or visit, as grandchildren include them in life events, or as great-grandchildren ensure that the family name will be carried on. Remembering activities of the past (part I, C)–a high bowling average, proficiency on a musical instrument, travels–may also bring joy. Current interests–gardening outdoors or indoors, reading, working crossword puzzles, watching birds, watching the evening news, surfing the Internet, telling jokes to friends–can also contribute to happiness. As we visit, I remind seniors that God wants them to be happy and that God provides interests and activities for them.

When I ask senior adults, "What are your three greatest strengths?" (part I, D) and "What are your major accomplishments in life?" (part I, E), they may need encouragement to respond positively if they were raised to be "humble" or if they are unaccustomed to self-analysis. I gently remind them that God has created each person with strengths and talents. Their initial response may refer to a skill, such as making repairs around the house or doing needlework. But as they become more introspective, they may mention that they have learned to say "I love you" to family members, have learned to allow themselves to cry in front of other people, or have learned to help other people with no thought of compensation. Frequently, however, senior adults will state (with a deep sense of pride) that their greatest strength is being able to live independently and to remain self-reliant.

In my follow-up ministry with the Smiths, I found it important to ask, "What are your greatest strengths?" As they adjusted to their post-stroke lives, recalling strengths that had brought them success in earlier years helped them use those strengths to adjust to lifestyle changes. Spencer's academic bent was focused on a new quest for learning as he devoured books on the topics of strokes and anger. He also put his well-developed self-discipline to work as he started occupational therapy with a home-health aide and practiced those lessons between sessions. Marcella used her organizational strengths and her love for people to organize monthly gatherings of friends in their home to lessen the social isolation they both felt. I also encouraged Marcella and Spencer to continue their spiritual discipline. As they meditated their way through the Spiritual Journey Exercise for Individuals (appendix A), they decided to videotape their answers and send the tape to their daughter as a way of sharing their legacy of faith with her.

If I observe items in senior adults' homes that may have special significance, I ask, "What treasured keepsakes are most important to you? What meaning do they have?" (part I, F). Photographs may lead to discussions about family and family events that may remind them of happy times (a picture from a wedding anniversary) or occasions when they and their family members were able to get through a difficult experience together (a picture of the first Christmas gathering without a deceased loved one). Decorative items on shelves may have been acquired at a significant point in their lives or may have been gifts from close friends or relatives. Talking about keepsakes can help senior adults recall meaningful life experiences and people who influenced their lives. The Smiths had so many keepsakes on display in their living room that I chose to focus on one or two periodically in the course of visitation. As I did so, these memories became additional sources of comfort for Marcella and Spencer.

II. Stress Level

Most difficult or unhappy situation. As I inquire about the most difficult or unhappy situation in senior adults' lives (part II, A), I also ask how they coped. I later record notes about these coping methods so that when they encounter future stressful situations, I can help them recall what helped in the past. When I did this with the Smiths, they said Spencer's stroke had been their most difficult situation, and faith was their greatest coping mechanism.

Elderly people may experience many forms of stress related to aging. Some of this stress may overlap with other components of the Parish Spiritual Assessment Tool, such as medical concerns. Joel said, "I can't do everything I want to do because my ankles are weak and I can't see well.

I know that if I did not have a home-health aide to help me with bathing and a housekeeper to take care of my house, I would have to move to a nursing home." Hazel laments, "I see my friends, who were once so vital, now become invalids and sometimes die. It's so sad, especially when I know that it's happening to me also." Marie states, "I have trouble sleeping at night because I know that if there was a fire I would be unable to get into my wheelchair in time to get out of the house and save myself."

Family issues may also cause great distress and significant depression for senior adults. Such concerns may include an adult child's divorce; dangerous employment (law enforcement officer, electrical worker, or over-the-road truck driver); an addiction to alcohol or drugs that may jeopardize the son's or daughter's health as well as ruin family celebrations; illness or disease (such as terminal cancer or early-onset Alzheimer's disease); or death (if seniors are unable to attend funerals, they cannot say good-bye to their loved ones). Although the Smiths said they did not want their daughter to give up her career and move home to help them, they also were depressed because she lived so far away. Stress may result also from the retirement of a spouse, creating the need for both spouses to adjust to being home together during the day. Especially stressful is the death of a spouse, along with the adjustment issues related to becoming a single person.

Elder abuse. Another source of stress for senior adults is past or current physical or verbal abuse. The caregiver needs to ask directly, "Have you been physically or verbally abused as a child or adult? If so, would you like to talk about it? Are you being abused now? If so, would it be helpful to talk about it?" (part II, B, C). The caregiver also needs to be aware of personal experiences and feelings in this area. If the caregiver is uncomfortable with this topic of discussion or has no experience with abuse victims, it may be advisable not to engage in it rather than to raise the subject and immediately drop it, say the wrong thing, or give a false expectation of help for the victim. If a senior adult raises the topic and the caregiver is unable to respond appropriately, the caregiver should bring in a resource person to assist. It is important to remember that when older people disclose past experiences of abuse, it may be the first time that they have talked about it, because such a topic of conversation in past years may have been taboo both in society and in the church.

If an older parishioner discloses current physical or verbal abuse, the perpetrator may be an adult child, a home-health care provider, a neighbor, or an angry spouse (whether the angry spouse is an invalid or an invalid's caregiver). Such disclosure needs to be viewed as a cry for help. Elder abuse calls for immediate response, assessment, and planning to protect the victim. It is crucial that abused senior adults hear the pastor or other caregiver state that abuse is unacceptable, often illegal, and always contrary to the will of God. Situations of elder abuse may need to be reported to governmental authorities. More will be said in chapter 4 about vulnerable adults.

Nighttime fears. Another possible area of stress is raised when I inquire, "Do you feel safe at night? If not, what do you fear?" (part II, D). Here again, when the caregiver asks such a question, she or he must be prepared to take action and to respond appropriately for the safety of senior adults. Some senior adults fear burglary or vandalism (and may have been victims of these crimes). When this is the case, the follow-up plan can include having door locks changed and locks installed on windows. If senior adults fear drug users and dealers who live next door, the assessment and plan can include telephoning the police and asking for extra patrols. Other nighttime fears for which assessment and planning are needed may include fear of falling when using the bathroom and not being able to get up again, fear that the home electric oxygen unit will not function if the electricity goes out, a fear of ruminating thoughts, a fear of not being able to reach or use the telephone to call for help if one has a stroke or heart attack, or a fear of how long it might be before the discovery of one's body if the senior adult should die while sleeping.

Weather. Weather may be another cause of stress. The caregiver should ask, "How do you feel in inclement weather?" and "If you are frightened, how do you deal with your fear?" (part II, D). While Spencer Smith had no fear because he knew Marcella could help him, disabled single people may not be able to walk down the basement stairs during a tornado warning. Other aging people who have limited lung capacity may have trouble breathing in extreme heat and humidity. Not only do they become homebound in summer because they need to remain in their air-conditioned homes, but they fear power outages that can leave them without safe air to breathe. Still other homebound members may have no one to remove snow from the front door. They may be literally "snowed in." The caregiver may develop a list of senior adults who need help during and after bad weather as well as a list of helpers who can check on their safety.

Alzheimer's disease. When I ask, "How much do you fear getting Alzheimer's?" (part II, F), I am aware that this can be one of the greatest areas of emotional stress for senior adults, especially those who have or have had loved ones with Alzheimer's disease. It is not unusual for senior adults to worry that normal forgetfulness is a sign of Alzheimer's disease. Some work to delay or prevent cognitive loss by challenging their minds with daily crossword puzzles, watching mind-challenging game shows on television, continuing to handle their own finances, playing board games or card games, and reading. Senior adults whose cognition begins to diminish are frequently aware of the change, may become frustrated that they can no longer think clearly, and may become fearful of what the changes might mean for the future, such as becoming a burden to loved ones or being placed in a nursing home.

Questions and misinformation abound about Alzheimer's (part II, G). The pastor or other caregiver needs to know where to obtain information about the disease (and preferably have resources for distribution available in the church office), where and when the nearest Alzheimer's support group meets, and where to find reputable Alzheimer's units in skilled-care facilities.

It is also important to encourage senior adults and their families to seek an accurate medical diagnosis. Sometimes a diagnosis other than Alzheimer's (but with similar symptoms) will be made. These can include affective disorder, anxiety, adjustment disorder, or late-onset psychosis. Cognitive impairment also can be caused by medications (both prescribed and over-the-counter) that may need to be changed or the dosage reduced, or by such medical problems as liver failure, kidney failure, dehydration, or infections of the central nervous system.[1] Even though the diagnosis may be difficult to ascertain, a medical treatment plan can usually be developed that will at least help senior adults and their families to cope emotionally.

III. Loneliness

Age-related changes in human relationships also may increase senior adults' feelings of loneliness and isolation. These changes may include loss of contact with co-workers after retirement, deaths of loved ones, reduced contact with adult children who are immersed in careers or child-raising, deterioration of physical health, or disability.

When senior adults are lonely, I encourage them to take control of how they deal with loneliness (this was my plan with the Smiths). The assessment tool section on loneliness (part III, section B) includes 18 possible ways to do this. Many of these strategies can be practiced by one who is homebound. For example, by cultivating a relationship with God through prayer and Bible-reading, one may become more aware of God's presence and may learn to enjoy and be content with one's own company. Isolated people may also take control of their loneliness by asking, "What are my interests? What stimulates and renews me?" They may decide to engage in one interest or more each day as a way not only of passing the time but also of filling time with worthwhile pursuits. They may reach out to other people, talk with them, and enjoy their company. Enjoying nature helps some to take control of loneliness. Watching changing cloud formations may be intriguing and may challenge the watcher to try to forecast the weather. Pets may add joy to their lives. If they cannot take care of a dog or cat, pets such as birds, turtles, and goldfish are fairly low-maintenance. Even a stuffed animal can provide some of the same benefits as a real animal, including huggability.

IV. Depression

While senior adults' loneliness may be due to a lack of companionship, depression goes deeper and should be handled differently by caregivers. Depression is more than just feeling "blue" or "down." Depressed senior adults may feel overwhelmed with the necessary activities and decisions of daily life, may lack self-esteem, and may be without hope. They may identify with Jesus' cry on the cross: "My God, my God, why have you forsaken me?" (Matt. 27:46).

As for all people, depression in senior adults has many causes. Age-related causes may include: multiple experiences of age-related deteriorating organ systems, diminished physical capabilities, changes in living situations, biochemical imbalance, physical illness or disease, prescription or over-the-counter medications, Alzheimer's disease, fear of Alzheimer's disease, decreased social support, multiple experiences of loss and grief (including loss of dignity and self-reliance), financial distress, spiritual distress because of an inability to attend worship and other church activities, lack of meaning in life, worry about the dying process and its duration and possible pain, and concern for eternal salvation.

Unfortunately, depression often remains undiagnosed in senior adults. People around them (including family and physicians) may say, "Oh, she's just sad and lonely. That's what happens when a person gets old." Such an attitude is unfortunate because depression is treatable in the elderly, just as it is in younger people.

As I initiate a discussion on depression, I ask, "Do you feel as much pleasure in life as you used to?" and "Do the things that used to make you happy still do so? If not, how often do you feel in a low mood?" (part IV, A). While these questions, in essence, ask the senior adult if she is depressed, they are phrased in a way that usually encourages her to participate more fully in such a discussion than if I had asked, "Are you depressed?" Sometimes a direct approach is appropriate, but when the senior adult is not accustomed to talking about depression or sharing depressed feelings, the less threatening approach seems to work more effectively.

When the senior adult indicates that she experiences what might be depression, I ask, "How do you deal with a low mood?" (part IV, B). If she is able to identify coping mechanisms, I affirm her use of effective methods. If she is unaware of how she deals with depression or does not know how to deal with it, I say, "Sometimes people deal with a low mood by talking with a friend, praying, or doing something to keep busy and interested in life. At other times people are unable to do anything but sit and stare and withdraw into themselves. Still others go to a professional therapist who helps them. Some of these ways help and some don't. Do you deal with your depression in any of these ways?" By raising both positive and negative ways of dealing with depression, I am usually more likely to learn how she copes. If she responds with unhealthy methods, I suggest alternative positive methods instead.

"Have you recently experienced changes in your sleep patterns or eating habits?" (part IV, C) is another question to ask. If the respondent has trouble sleeping or if her eating habits have changed, my follow-up question may be, "Have you ever felt that life was not worth living?" (part IV, D). If the senior adult says that has been a part of her past experience, I ask, "Did you receive professional help at that time?" If she did, I also ask, "What helped you the most to get through that time?" I encourage her to apply those skills to her current episode of depression. If she did not receive professional help, we attempt to identify inner resources that may have helped her in the past so that she can apply them now.

If she states that life is not worth living, I directly ask, "Are you feeling suicidal?" (part IV, E). If she is, I invite her to her to talk about her suicidal feelings and about what is distressing in her life. It is imperative to be a good listener, not to contradict her feelings, to offer reassurance of her importance to those around her, to affirm the sustaining presence of God who strengthened her in the past and will continue to do so now, and to assure her of my concern and support.

As she talks about her suicidal feelings, I also ask, "Do you have a plan for ending your life?" (part IV, E). If she has a plausible plan (and sometimes even if she does not), I immediately seek professional help (part IV, E). If the caregiver is a layperson, she or he may want to telephone the pastor for assistance. If the caregiver is the pastor, she or he may ask the senior adult for permission to telephone her family to assist in taking her to a professional therapist or hospital emergency room. If no family member is available, I take the senior adult there myself. If the pastor or other caregiver is uncertain whether immediate action is called for, remember that it important to err on the side of caution rather than to take the risk that the senior adult will end her life.

V. Perspective on Aging

The purpose of "Perspective on Aging" (part V) is to encourage senior adults to reflect on what the aging process means for them. I find that these questions are often of great interest. In fact, respondents usually answer them eagerly, spontaneously illustrating them with anecdotes. I also find that when these questions are taken in order, senior adults can hardly wait to hear the next question. I always preface this discussion by telling them that they can choose not to answer any question. That happens infrequently.

When I ask, "What are the best things about your age now?" (part V, A), they usually restate the question and say, "I haven't thought about the best things about getting old before!" Following a short pause, they quickly answer. Sophia gently said, "I think the best thing is that my children and grandchildren are where they should be in life. They are doing so well. And I like it when they come and see me!" Cora rejoiced as she said, "I'm glad I can be up and about. My health is good. I can even do my housework! Plus, I raise geraniums indoors in the winter." Judith's eyes twinkled as she said, "I'm 92 years old and have learned how to do E-mail. I E-mailed my grandson on his birthday, and he was so surprised! It was fun!" This question, indeed, challenges senior adults to realize that there are positive aspects to growing older.

When I ask the next question, "What do you hope for as you grow older?" (part V, B), senior adults sometimes restate the question before responding in such words as, "I've never thought there might be something positive in the future." Yet, they quickly think of something and state the answer with almost a tone of surprise that the future can be hopeful. This question helps senior adults to reflect on their future and helps the caregiver to understand some of their greatest desires. Sometimes the assessment and plan can incorporate ways to assist senior adults to work toward the fulfillment of their hope.

Senior adults usually take time to ponder the next two questions. Responses to the question, "What is the most difficult part of growing old?" (part V, C) may include statements about needing to depend on other people in new ways, worrying about being confined to a wheelchair, seeing friends become forgetful and blind, or being concerned about developing Alzheimer's. Responses to the question, "What do you hope you will never need to give up?" (part V, D) may be related. Common, poignant responses include "my apartment or home," "my faith," "my mind," "my eyes," or "my children to death." Again, these responses are often accompanied with illustrations from immediate experience–what it was like to see a friend become forgetful, blind, or confined to a wheelchair. Vivid stories about placing a spouse or parent in a nursing home may accompany a response about the fear of giving up an apartment or home. If a senior adult hopes she will never have to give up her faith, the illustration may relate to a friend who in old age became bitter and gave up on God. Anecdotes about friends and relatives with Alzheimer's abound for senior adults who hope they will not lose their mind to the dread disease.

The next question, "What is your secret to living a long life?" (part V, E) can be fun, and the senior adult may respond with a sense of pride.

Dora declared, "Be your own doctor. I know my own body better than the doctors do!"

Selmer said, "I tried to take care of my health when I was younger, even when I had dirty working conditions, but if I had known I would live this long I would have taken even better care of myself!"

Ramona said, "Trust in God and take everything to God in prayer. Then listen to what God tells you."

Mitchell replied, "Read your Bible and pray every day. Don't let yourself worry. Take it to the Lord in prayer and leave it there."

Victor quickly and animatedly said, "Be active. Go fishing! Don't overeat!"

Myra said, "Try to be happy every day and look forward to heaven!"

As a way of celebrating the long life of the senior adult, the caregiver may wish to discuss each response more fully if there is time.

When I ask senior adults, "What is the biggest change you have experienced in your lifetime?" (part V, F), they respond either on a personal or a historical level. When the response is personal, they may refer to the birth or death of children or grandchildren, the death of a spouse or close friend, a chronic disease that created lifelong physical limitations, the experience of becoming homebound, or having to move to a retirement facility. Historical responses may include the change from automobiles without doors to automobiles with doors and telephones; refrigeration that allows meat to be kept for long periods of time, eliminating the need to get fresh meat every day; the greater cleanliness and personal hygiene possible with hot running water; not having to share bathwater with others; less healthy processed food and fast food compared to the wholesome food of the past; the radio that brought music including hymns and opera into their homes; television, which brought the world closer through the news; electric lights, which reduced the number of house fires caused by burning candles; and automatic bank deposits. Again, the questioner may wish to pursue these areas in more depth, as a way of affirming the senior adults' experiences.

Asking senior adults, "If you could share words of wisdom with younger people, what would you share?" (part V, G) suggests that the caregiver believes that they are wise, affirms them for who they are, and acknowledges their worth. Their responses are usually words of wisdom from which everyone can benefit. For example, when we celebrated Tilda's 100th birthday and I asked her that question, she quickly and emphatically stated, "Do everything that is right according to God's will for you!" Others have made the following statements:

"Stay in school. Get a good education."

"Respect people who earn your respect."

"Remember to pray every day, and believe that God always answers your prayers–because God does!"

"Listen to your heart!"

"Count your blessings every day."

VI. Support

The two reasons for including "Support" (part VI) are directly related to the caregiver's ability to assess and plan for the needs of senior adults. First, it is important for the caregiver to know how much psychological support is available to the senior adult. Second, it is important to know who is in the person's network of support so that if the caregiver needs to enlist help in caring for the senior adult, these people can be contacted.

Helping the Smiths Regain Power and Feelings of Independence

Even before I left Marcella and Spencer's home, I was pleased that I had time to begin my assessment and plan with them. They needed to know that there was help for their stressful situation. Consulting my schedule of afternoon visits, I saw that we could get started with a plan before I needed to leave for the next visit. I also knew that they were capable of contacting church and community resources.

Assessment and Plan

I. Professional Objectivity
  A. How do I feel about these senior adults? I like them and feel frustrated along with them about their changing life situation.
  B. Do they have life issues that are similar to mine that would make it difficult for me to be objective? No.
  C. Do I have countertransference issues? If so, what are they? I may tend to empathize too closely as I wonder how I would handle a similar situation if my active life came to an abrupt halt.
  D. Do they have transference issues? If so, what are they? I need to be careful so that my assessment and plan do not lead them to view me as their physician rather than as their pastor.

II. Senior Adult's Agenda
  A. What do these senior adults want?
    1. Spiritually: To receive home communion. Marcella also wants to return to her monthly circle meetings.
    2. Psychologically: Both of them want to learn how to handle their new situation so that they can be happy again. Marcella wants to relieve her loneliness by attending her garden club and circle meetings. Spencer wants to learn how to handle his anger constructively.
    3. Familially: They do not want this situation to affect their marriage relationship adversely. They also do not want their daughter to feel guilty and move home.
    4. Socioeconomically: They want to use some of their savings to avoid nursing home placement.

5. Medically: Both of them want to prevent injuries to Marcella that could occur as she assists Spencer. Spencer also wants to need less physical assistance from Marcella. He wants to walk again.

III. Pastor's or Other Caregiver's Assessment

A. Spiritual

1. Assessment: They need regularly scheduled home communion and lay visitation. Marcella also needs to attend her circle meetings.
2. Ways to foster growth: Tell them I will bring them home communion on a regular basis. Refer them to the Stephen Ministries program. Find someone to stay with Spencer so that Marcella feels free to attend circle meetings.

B. Psychological

1. Assessment: Both Marcella and Spencer are lonely and depressed.
2. Ways to foster growth: Listen to their feelings. Tell them I will help them find ways for Marcella to attend garden club and circle meetings. Encourage them to use their organizational skills to invite friends to their home. Help Spencer find resource people who can help him understand and learn how to handle his anger and who can assist him with bathing so that he does not have to be so dependent on Marcella.

C. Family

1. Assessment: In-home services (including some from the church) may enable Marcella and Spencer to view each other more as equals again, each with a separate identity, even though Spencer will always need Marcella's help for the activities of daily life. As they explain these services to their daughter, they will be able to tell her that they can take care of themselves (so that she will not feel a need to move home to take care of them).
2. Way to foster growth: Follow through with referral information about in-home services.

D. Socioeconomic

1. Assessment: They have the financial means to provide the in-home services. Later they may need suggestions for how to spend time at home and how to socialize with others.

2. Ways to foster growth: During a future visit, offer to explore suggestions for how to spend time at home and how to socialize with others, per the socioeconomic component (parts IV and V).

E. Medical
1. Assessment: They need home health services. They also need someone for housecleaning and yard work.
2. Way to foster growth: Refer them to the appropriate community resource agencies.

IV. Plan for Responding to the Senior Adult's Needs

A. What church resources are available to address Marcella and Spencer's needs? The pastor (me) and the Stephen Ministries program.
1. Who is available to contact the Stephen Ministries coordinator? The pastor (me).
2. When will the contact be made? Tomorrow morning when I am in the office.
3. When will the plan be implemented? As soon as the coordinator can find a lay visitor who is able to visit on a regular basis and who is able to visit with Spencer when Marcella needs to attend her circle meeting (and perhaps when she attends her garden club meetings).
4. Date on which to provide for follow-up: I will write a note to myself to contact the Stephen Ministries coordinator in two weeks.

B. What community resources are available to address their needs? A home-health agency (for bathing, housecleaning, and educating Marcella about proper ways to help transfer and lift Spencer, as well as educating Spencer about dealing with his anger) and the senior citizen center (for volunteers who do yard work).
1. Who is available to contact the resources? I will ask the office manager to contact Marcella with these telephone numbers. Marcella is capable of making the calls.
2. When will the contact be made? The office manager will contact Marcella tomorrow morning. It will be up to Marcella to telephone the resources.
3. When will the plan be implemented? When Marcella gets it accomplished.

4. Date on which to provide for follow-up. In addition to calling the Stephen Ministries coordinator in two weeks, I will also call Marcella and Spencer to schedule my next communion visit and to see if they need further help with in-home services.

V. Likely Consequences if I Elect to Do Less or More than Expected or Needed

A. Spiritual consequences: If I do not follow up with regular home communion visits, connect them with a lay visitor, or make it possible for Marcella to attend her circle meetings, they may have no contact with their church and their faith may waiver.

B. Psychological consequences: Since part of their depression is caused by stroke-related life changes, if I do not help them find the appropriate in-home resources, their depression may intensify. If I make the telephone calls for them (to the home-health agency and the senior citizen center), I will diminish their power at a time when they are already feeling powerless. Encouraging them to invite friends to their home can empower them. They will feel less depressed if they can regain some control over their lives again.

C. Family consequences: If I do not respond according to plan, their marital relationship may become more strained, and it may affect their daughter's career if she decides to move home.

D. Socioeconomic consequences: None regarding home-health services. This is their choice. If I give them suggestions for how to spend time at home and how to socialize with others now, they may feel even more overwhelmed than they do already. There will be time for this later.

E. Medical consequences: If I do not refer them to home-health services, Marcella's health may deteriorate and they may fail to increase their knowledge about dealing with strokes.

This was just the beginning of a new lifestyle for Marcella and Spencer. As the plan for bringing in home-health services was implemented, they learned new skills for handling this major change. It was important for them to "take charge," because both Marcella and Spencer were retired professionals gifted with organizational skills. As they took control, their depression eased.

When Marcella was able to resume her circle and garden club meetings, her mood lifted. I continued to bring them home communion, for which they always set their dining-room table as a home altar, complete with candles, special cloth, and cross. The Stephen Ministries coordinator found two lay visitors. One exclusively provided visitation. The other became almost a transportation coordinator as he visited with Spencer when Marcella attended her various meetings and as he assisted Spencer to leave the house occasionally to attend communion at church.

Marcella and Spencer continue to struggle with life changes. Yet as they do so, they feel more empowered and in control despite limitations. They will probably always struggle with some level of depression, but life no longer seems hopeless. They have planned their first home social gathering. They are now trying to figure out how to attend local stroke support group meetings together. Knowing them, I am sure they will figure it out!

CHAPTER 4

Senior Adults' Family Dynamics

Raymond: Fear of Losing the Family Legacy

Thanks to a referral from a member of the senior advisory committee, 79-year-old Raymond had not "fallen though the cracks" of our visitation program. This could easily have happened because ever since his wife died nine years ago, he had been nearly invisible in our congregation. The memory of the two of them regularly attending worship was almost too painful for Raymond to bear. He now attended only a few times a year. He made sure that those were communion Sundays. His four daughters cannot attend worship with him because they live in other communities; they and their families are members of other churches. Because of the changes in Raymond's life, as well as in the congregation's lay and pastoral leadership, Raymond could have become a lost sheep in our flock.

This was my second visit with Raymond. During our first visit, it did not take long to discover that Raymond is quiet and forgetful and that he needs extra time to formulate his thoughts and actions. His cognitive impairment is caused by a stroke he suffered seven months ago. As a result of the stroke, he can no longer drive a car, can move around his house only with the aid of a walker, and does not go outdoors unless one of his daughters is with him. (They have a weekly rotation schedule to visit and do his weekly chores.)

Raymond was receiving home communion for the first time. As I explained what to do during the service ("Just sit where you are, listen to my words, and pray silently along with me. I'll give you the bread and wine at the appropriate times"), he slowly said, "After my stroke, I never thought I'd get communion again. I still can't believe that you will come to my house and do this."

At the start of our second visit, he began talking about the daughter who was coming the next day. As he told me about her and other family members, I used the family component as a way of bringing deeper meaning to our conversation. This worked well, and he seemed to enjoy it. When I asked him what values he and his wife had tried to pass on to his daughters, he emphatically stated, "We wanted them to learn to believe in God, be active in church, and work hard." When I asked him what values his parents had passed on to him, I was not surprised to hear him say, "To believe in God, to go to church every Sunday you can get there, and to work hard."

As he spoke about his parents, it was evident that they had been loving people who were still very important to him. He was only 35 when his father died in an automobile accident. His mother had died a year earlier of a heart attack. When I asked, "What effect did their deaths have on you?" he began to cry quietly and to talk about the love with which he and his four brothers had been raised. He said that his biggest regret after his parents died was not being able to take his teenage daughters to visit them. He tearfully continued, "Before I die, I want to tell my daughters more about their grandparents. If I can tell them, they can tell my grandchildren, and one day they [the grandchildren] can tell their children. But I'm afraid if I try to talk to them, I'll cry–because I still miss my folks so much. If I cry when I talk to my daughters, they'll feel sad because I will be sad. The last thing I want is for them to be sad.

Because I needed to maintain my afternoon schedule of visits and still needed to give Raymond communion, I was disappointed that I needed to bring closure to our session. After I summarized our conversation and again acknowledged his feelings, I asked him if he would like me to return next Wednesday afternoon at 2:00 P.M. so that we could further discuss how he could talk to his daughters. He said he would like that.

Family Issues

While this component is not meant to be a description of family systems theory, it is intended to be a practical way to talk with senior adults about their families, whether or not they have surviving family members. When senior adults initiate a discussion about their families, those who have been married will often begin with spouse and children. This was true for Raymond. The discussion questions in parts IV and V ("Marital Status" and "Children") can be used by the pastor or other caregiver to guide senior adults into conversations that go beyond the basic information about how long they have been married and how many children they have. Following this conversation, I use the family component outline to invite older adults to discuss their childhood, parents, and siblings–areas they usually have little opportunity to talk about.

When I, rather than the senior adults, initiate a discussion about their families, I usually invite them to begin by talking about their childhood, parents, and siblings. I like to begin with early family history, because while not all senior adults have been married or have children, yet all have had childhood experiences and parents. Sometimes they also have siblings. As I learn about their early years, I am better able to help them draw connections between their childhood family relationships and their current relationships. As we make these connections, senior adults frequently develop new insights about what has been and continues to be meaningful about their families. We also discuss marital status and children, when applicable. This process is helpful not only to senior adults, but it is also intriguing for me professionally as I develop an understanding of how the senior adults' early family experiences continue to shape them.

More than one visit about family history is usually needed to complete the family component. At the conclusion of each visit, I enter the information into my laptop computer so that I can refer to it as needed. While some senior adults enjoy engaging in frequent conversations about their families (which helps me remember information), others believe that once they have shared this information, I will remember it, so there is no need to talk about it again unless something special comes up. With the numbers of visits I make, I find it impossible (at least initially) to remember all the family relationships and dynamics. As senior adults' family dynamics change, I update my records. Rather than relying on my memory, I rely on the memory of my laptop.

Having this information readily available is important for other reasons as well. First, it is helpful to have the name and telephone number of a family member. If the senior adult needs home-health services, physician consultation, additional groceries, meals-on-wheels, or medication evaluation, and he is unable to make arrangements for help himself, a telephone call by me to a family member may be all that is needed to obtain family assistance. However, if the family member is unavailable or unwilling to help, I develop an assessment and plan to ensure that the senior adult is cared for appropriately and in a timely way.

Second, in situations of advancing dementia, having a family member to call can be important for the senior adult's safety and well-being. Sometimes symptoms may not be immediately recognizable by family members who live far away or who are immersed in their own families or careers. In such situations, I may be the first person who notices the changes. Again, if enlisting immediate assistance from a family member is not an option, I develop another assessment and plan.

Third, in other situations when I wonder "who is related to whom," it is helpful to be able to refer to my notes. When I learn that a member of the congregation has a serious problem (such as cancer or a critical accident), I may wonder if a senior adult in the family may be worried and in need of pastoral care. And when a senior adult is unable to attend family baptisms, confirmations, weddings, or funerals, a visit to the aged family member may be welcomed.

I. Childhood

While senior adults usually feel pleased to be asked, "Where were you born and raised?" (part I, A), the question also may so surprise them that they rephrase it to make sure they heard correctly: "You want to know where I was born and raised?" It may seem almost too good to be true that someone is interested in this part of their life. I respond, "Yes, I do. Your early years have greatly influenced who you are today."

I often find that it is unnecessary to ask the next questions, "What was your childhood like?" and "By whom were you primarily raised?" (part I, B, C). Those I visit are usually eager to talk about their childhood experiences–and often to place their experiences in the context of faith.

Sometimes when older people do not spontaneously talk about their childhood, their reticence is an indication of childhood crises. After I ask, "What was your childhood like?" and "Did you experience major crises as a child?" (part I, D), they may relate stories about being raised by only one parent or by people other than their biological parents, such as grandparents, aunts and uncles, or neighbors. As we visit, we explore the inner strength that God gave them in their earlier years, and we talk about how that strength helps them now that they are retired or disabled.

II. Parents

"Are your parents still living?" (part II, A) may seem a strange question to ask elderly people, yet sometimes they do have living parents. This point is congruent with the United States Administration on Aging's report, which states that the number of aged people is increasing. In 1997, the 65-74 age group (18.5 million) was eight times larger than in 1900, the 75-84 group (11.7 million) was 16 times larger, and the 85-plus group (3.9 million) was 31 times larger.[1] Newly retired senior adults of 65 may have parents who are 85 or older. Men and women at age 75 with their own physical limitations may have parents with even more limitations. And people who have reached the age of 100 or older may have 80-year-old sons or daughters who live in nursing homes.

Thus, the next question, "If so, are you their caretaker?" (part II, B) may be answered affirmatively. Senior adults may take care of their parents' needs for medical and psychological care, shopping, and assistance with finances. They also may try to care for parents' spiritual needs by taking them to church or calling the pastor to bring communion. Some active senior adults take care of their parents' needs themselves, or (if they have limited time or energy) may employ someone else to help. Seniors taking care of parents will become even more common in future years as baby boomers continue to age.

Older adults whose parents have died, on the other hand, may still need to grieve. One poignant effect which parents' deaths can have on senior adults (part II, C, D, E) was described in the opening story of this chapter. Although Raymond's parents died more than 40 years ago, he still grieves their deaths, experiences their love, and wants their values to continue in his family. Thus, whether parents have died or are still alive, the senior adult continues to be powerfully affected by parental lives–whether in positive or negative ways.

Whether senior adults had positive or negative relationships with their parents, they usually learned lessons for life from them. Asking, "What did you learn from your parents?" (part II, F) may therefore help the respondent articulate those lessons.

LaVonne said, "I learned what sacrificial love is from my mother because she always sacrificed her own needs and wants for the sake of us children."

Belinda said, "From my mother I learned how important it is to help other people."

John said, "I learned how not to treat my children. Even though I was tempted, I never laid a hand on my children because I know how deep those emotional scars still are for me from my father's beatings."

III. Siblings

Perhaps one of the least discussed areas of senior adult family dynamics is that of sibling relationships. This omission may be due to the time constraints of visits, oversight, or failure to realize siblings' importance. Even the lack of sibling relationships can be significant for senior adults, as can step-sibling relationships.

Sometimes sibling relationships are cherished as wonderful sources of support. At other times, however, they can create stress. Fern wanted to help her brother but did not know how. She said, "The doctor told my brother that he needs cataract surgery. I can't take him to the nearest city to have it done, because I'm afraid to drive in traffic. I don't know what to do."

In another situation, Everett, who had always been close to his twin sister, Evelyn, did not realize that it was his sister's dementia that led her to tell him, "I don't like you anymore. You are not a nice person. I don't have to talk to you, and I don't want to talk to you anymore."

In situations such as these, the caregiver's assessment and plan can include education and referral. Fern can be informed about the transportation services she and her brother could use to travel to an eye clinic. Everett can be informed about symptoms of dementia and possibly referred to an Alzheimer's support group, where he can learn more about dementia and receive support from others in similar situations.

Deaths of siblings, even in the distant past, can be stressful in the present. Audrey lamented, "I've always felt guilty that my brother died as he was saving me from drowning when we were children."

Ed said, "I had five sisters and three brothers. Who would have thought that I, the second-oldest, would be the last one left in my family! I feel so alone–and I am alone."

Emma's eyes filled with tears as she said, "My sister, who lives in a nursing home 500 miles from here, is dying. I want to tell her how much I love her, but she's so hard of hearing now that she can't hear me when I call. I won't even be able to attend her funeral because I'm in a wheelchair and have no one to fly on an airplane with me."

Milton, an only child, speculated, "I've always wondered what it would be like to have a brother or sister. I'm totally alone in the world. I don't even know who will attend my funeral, since I have no family and my friends are all in the same shape I'm in."

In these situations the caregiver's assessment and plan may include encouraging these senior adult siblings to continue to share feelings and family history, and to invite them to talk about their own death and dying (by using part IX of the spiritual component).

In addition to one-on-one visitation, another ministry which I occasionally provide for sibling senior adults is that of transportation. I do this in situations in which one or both siblings no longer drive, are invalids, or have limited opportunities to visit and worship with one another. This was true when I gave semi-invalid Preston a ride to his invalid brother Paul's home. I also do this in situations in which a homebound sibling lives farther away than the other sibling feels comfortable driving. For example, I often invited Inga to join me when I drove 30 miles to bring her invalid sister, Velma, communion. Each time when we arrived, Velma, who had early-stage dementia, rushed up to Inga with a broad smile and repeatedly said, "Oh, Sis, it is so good to see you. I love you. I thought I'd never see you again. I'm so happy!"

IV. Marital Status

Married. A statement about marital status may be the most common way for many senior adults to initiate a discussion about family relationships (part IV, A). To the question, "How long have you been married?" they respond in a variety of ways. Some state that they have been married to the same person for 50, 60, or even nearly 70 years. Others say they only recently married or have been married more than once. Those who have remarried may indicate the number of years they were married each time and talk about each relationship. On the whole, statistics indicate that older men are more likely to be married than older women. In 1997, among older adults 74 percent of men and 42 percent of women were married.[2]

As I inquire, "Where were you married?" senior adults often volunteer other information as well, such as their denominational background, worship preferences, and theology.

Although married people may respond quickly to the question, "Have you celebrated any special anniversaries or events?" they may need more time to ponder the next question, "How has God been part of your marriage?" I inquire about God's role in their marriage in order to invite them to explore a theological meaning in their relationship. Answers to this thought-provoking question vary. Couples may state that God has been a part of their marriage because they were married in a church, they had their children baptized and educated in the church, they attended church regularly, or they pray together.

Every pastor and caregiver knows that the senior adult population includes more widows than widowers. In fact, in 1997 there were four times as many widows (8.5 million) as widowers (2.1 million), and almost half (46 percent) of all older women were widows.[3] Both widows and widowers have usually been forced to make difficult adjustments. The pastor or other caregiver who invites them to talk in depth about their experience provides a sensitive and meaningful ministry.

The surviving spouse may have had few opportunities to talk about the grief experience after the loved one's death. Questions such as "How long ago did your spouse die?" and "Where did you spouse die?" (part IV, B) can begin the process. Deaths that occurred at home may be especially traumatic, particularly if the spouse died in the marriage bed, sitting in a chair next to the survivor, or at the kitchen table while they were eating a meal.

Survivors whose spouses died after an extended illness perceive the length of the dying process in different ways. One survivor may have valued that time as a way to "put our house in order," while another may continue to grieve because the long dying process meant that both spouses suffered greatly because of their helplessness.

Survivors whose spouses died suddenly also view the nature of the death in various ways. It may have been perceived as an almost unbearable shock to one survivor, yet it may have been viewed as a blessing to another, especially if the deceased had talked about not wanting to linger in death. As the caregiver asks what helped the surviving spouse work through the grief, an assessment and plan about further grief work can be made.

If the deceased spouse had Alzheimer's, it is important to invite the survivor to talk about what that disease was like for both of them. These questions can facilitate the discussion: "Did your spouse have Alzheimer's or some form of dementia?" and "Were you a caretaker for your spouse? If so, for how long?" Undoubtedly if the spouse had Alzheimer's, it was a difficult experience. It might have meant any or all of the following for the caregiver partner: being verbally and physically abused, having sleep constantly interrupted by the spouse's confusion with time, helping the partner in the bathroom, being the target of thrown items, having one's statements misinterpreted, having to monitor the kitchen stove so the partner would not turn it on and leave it on, trying to keep clothing on one's spouse, fearing that the partner would get lost while driving or have an automobile accident, worrying that the spouse would become lost in the house (such as in the basement or attic) or would wander out of the house and get lost, and becoming socially isolated and homebound. The assessment and plan may include offering the survivor spouse the opportunity to talk further about these experiences, as well as affirming the dedication shown to the spouse.

The question "How have you made a new life for yourself?" will, one hopes, encourage widows and widowers to do just that, if they have not already done so. Sometimes survivors need encouragement to move on with their lives so that they can say, as Colleen did, "For the longest time after he died, I just stayed at home, did my housework and cooking, and a little needlework. But when our congregation formed a senior adult Lunch Bunch and the pastor invited me to attend, I decided to try it. As I went out to eat with others from the church, I realized how important it was to be with other people again. Now, I even occasionally go on a day trip with the senior citizen center."

Other survivors, however, are unable to move on with their lives. Olga, for example, said, "Albert and I were so close. After he was cremated, I had his ashes placed in a baseball-shaped urn–because he loved baseball. I turned one of the rooms in our house into a shrine for Albert. During baseball season I sit there in his favorite chair, look at all his baseball paraphernalia, and watch games. I feel close to him there. It's my favorite room in the house!" For Olga, who has been unable to move on with her life, the question "How have you made a new life for yourself?" can help her reflect at least on daily changes that she has already quietly made, such as cooking for one, eating alone, and making decisions without consulting her partner. Ideally, the question will encourage her to make other changes as well. This question may be an important one to ask Raymond at an appropriate time. The assessment and plan in these situations can include helping survivors to do additional grief work that may lead to positive changes in their lives.

Divorced. While divorced senior adults constituted only 7 percent of all older people in 1997, their numbers (2.2 million) have increased five times faster than the older population as a whole since 1990.[4] Causes of divorce for the elderly parallel those for younger persons. Some of these causes include alcohol-related problems, uncontrolled anger leading to verbal and sometimes physical abuse, financial stress, marital infidelity, disability resulting from dementia or accident or illness, and communication problems. While these dynamics lead to divorce for some senior adults, they are also present in other marriages in which divorce is desired but not considered an option. Some senior adults remain in difficult marriages because they have no one other than the estranged spouse to care for them physically or to support them financially. Some senior adults' religious beliefs preclude divorce, or they believe that divorce would be an embarrassment at their age.

The question "How do you feel about being divorced now?" (part IV, D) is intended to offer divorced senior adults pastoral care. They may have questions about the permanency of their marriage vows, Bible passages related to divorce and adultery, the church's view toward divorced people, or their relationship with God after divorce. Senior adults may welcome this question, especially if at the time of their divorce they or those around them treated divorce as a taboo subject. In some situations they may need to hear words of absolution, even many years after the divorce The assessment and plan may include follow-up conversations to deal with their thoughts and feelings about their divorce, as well as to affirm their personhood, their value to God, and their value to God's people.

Again, as with widows and widowers, the question "How have you made a new life for yourself?" encourages divorced people to believe that it is appropriate for them to be happy, to lead meaningful lives, and to make changes that can make such happiness possible. The development of strategies for assisting senior adults to do this can be incorporated into the assessment and plan.

Single, never married. Senior adults who have never married comprise 4 percent of the older-adult population.[5] Frequently they have developed careers and learned to be self-sufficient. Their answers vary greatly when I ask, "How do you feel about being single?" and "What led to your decision not to marry?" (part IV, D).

Doris responded, "As I grew up, my mother was a widow and was bedridden. She needed my physical and emotional support as well as my financial support, so I went to work. We lived together for 23 years until she died. Then I was so comfortable with my lifestyle that I never considered marriage."

LaVern shook his head from side to side as he said, "My folks could never get along. They were always at each other's throats. I decided I didn't want that to happen to me, so I didn't try marriage."

Tilda's eyes danced as she smiled and said, "I knew from early childhood that I wanted to be a teacher. I studied hard, and I enjoyed teaching. I influenced more children by being a teacher than I would have if I had had children of my own!"

Norris laughed as he said, "I was just too feisty to get married!"

The question "What opportunities have you had as a single person that you might not have experienced had you married?" (part IV, D) is frequently answered in fascinating ways.

Muriel told intriguing stories about her many travels to Europe and said that she could not have afforded to travel if she had married and had children.

Norma said, "I lived to bowl. I always used the newest and best bowling shoes and bowling balls. I bowled six nights a week and traveled to other states for tournaments. Let me show you my trophies!"

Carlyle matter-of-factly said, "I had the opportunity to rise in business and purchase my own company. This would not have been possible if I had married because I spent every last penny and every waking moment on my company. I knew I didn't have any leftover energy for a spouse or children."

V. Children

Who they are. While the questions "Do you have children?" and "How many?" (part V, A, B) can be answered with simple statements about the number of one's biological children, they can also lead to complex responses. For example, some senior adults may have foster children or stepchildren. Others may have legally adopted children. They may even have legally adopted grandchildren. Still other seniors may have legally adopted the children of their deceased siblings or cousins. In other situations, aging people may consider unrelated children–such as neighbor children whom they raised-to be their children, even if the children were never legally adopted. Thus, this seemingly simple question about the number of children can lead to complex responses.

Deceased. The questions "Are they [the children] all living?" and "If not, what was the circumstance of the death?" (part V, C) may lead to touching conversations. The death of a child is among the most painful forms of loss. It seems unnatural that those who are older should survive those who are younger. Seniors whose children died at an early age may still blame themselves if they believe they had a role in the child's death. This may be true if the death resulted from an accident caused by the parents or one that the parents were unable to prevent. It may also be true if the death resulted from a medical crisis for which they could not obtain timely medical care. These parents may wonder daily what their child would be like now if she or he had lived. If the child died in young adulthood, the cause of death may likewise continue to grieve senior adult parents, especially if the child was a murder victim, a war casualty, the victim of a drunk driver, a suicide, or the victim of a drug or alcohol overdose. The caregiver's assessment and plan may include ongoing grief work with the parents.

Senior adults whose child is dying need pastoral care. When they have the opportunity to be with their dying child, senior adult parents may feel helpless, especially if the son or daughter becomes emaciated or suffers greatly. In some situations, because of their own disabilities, the elderly parents may be unable to visit or care for the dying child. As they prepare for the death of their child, they may feel they need pastoral permission to pray for their child's death, especially if that is the only way they perceive for the child to be relieved of suffering. Such a prayer may be the greatest form of love. During the dying process, senior adult parents may also wonder anxiously whether they will be consulted by their son-in-law or daughter-in-law about funeral arrangements and whether they will be allowed to continue their relationship with their grandchildren after the death. The pastor or other caregiver's assessment and plan will need to address such fears.

Living. When senior adults have living children, asking "Where do your children live?" (part V, D) may enable the caregiver to make family connections. Then a more comprehensive family ministry can be offered if the children are also members of the congregation. The question may also help the caregiver develop an idea as to whether the children can easily be supportive, considering their geographic distance from their parents.

As the caregiver inquires, "What values have you attempted to pass on to your children?" (part V, E), the senior adults' responses will often relate both to faith and to practical aspects of daily living.

Javonne thoughtfully said, "I tried to raise my children to be loving people because Jesus said we should love our neighbors as ourselves."

Dana said, "Since my parents read the Bible to me every night at bedtime, I did the same for my children, hoping that it would become a part of their adult lives–and it has. One of my children has read the Bible four times, and one reads the Bible sometimes in her church on Sunday morning."

Palmer replied, "Faithfulness and loving the Lord is what I tried to pass on to my children, because that's the only way I was able to get through the trials of life!"

"Being an honest person is what I wanted my son to learn," Clara said.

Selmer replied, "My wife and I always had to work hard to keep food on the table. We instilled in our children the value and reward of a hard day's work."

Lavina grinned as she said, "I told them time and time again to save money, be fair, and be independent!"

Supportive. Pastors and other caregivers know that some senior adults are blessed with supportive children, while others struggle along with uninvolved sons and daughters. By phrasing the next question, "Are your children able and willing to help you with some of your needs now?" (part V, F) senior adults have the freedom to respond with examples of support, reasons their children are unable to help them, or examples of stress associated with adult children. Some senior adults receive from their adult children support that may include: relocation to the parents' community to care for them, an invitation to their parents to move in with them, frequent trips of two to four hours to the parents' home to do chores and caregiving, regular visits and telephone calls, in-home services such as meal preparation and housecleaning, help with finances and insurance forms, transportation, and emotional support.

Even though Raymond's daughters lived in other communities, they rotated their care for their father as one of them drove to his home each week. They cleaned his house, shopped for groceries, paid his bills, handled his insurance forms, and told him they loved him. When he had a medical appointment, one of them always came to take him there. They also scheduled themselves so that one daughter called him each morning and another each evening.

While senior adults such as Raymond experience comfort and love from supportive children, they can at the same time feel stress as they become dependent on their children's support. For example, some senior adults may worry that the supportive children will become ill and unable to help. Others fear that children may die while away on a business trip. Still others are concerned that their children may become worn out from caregiving. Some aging people fear that their children may retire to a warm climate and no longer be available to help them. Some may fear that if they admit that they become exhausted by visits with their children, the visits will be curtailed. It is unfortunate that the blessing of supportive children can become a cause of stress for aging people.

Unsupportive. Adult children have a variety of reasons for being uninvolved with their aging parents. These reasons can include unresolved feelings of anger related to earlier family conflicts, career commitments, geographic distance, commitment to spouse and children, marital stress, personal medical problems, unawareness of the parents' need, lack of initiative to inquire about parents' needs, or inability to accept that their parents are getting old.

Aging parents whose children are uninvolved may find birthdays and holidays especially lonely if they are not remembered. Sometimes adult children do not realize how important it is for grandparents to learn to know their grandchildren. Senior adults who are former citizens of a country in which the elderly are revered may experience deep disappointment when their Americanized children do not revere them as they revered their own parents. When children are short-tempered, senior adults may fear that if they say the wrong thing they will not be allowed either to see their grandchildren or to talk to them on the telephone. Perhaps the greatest despair is experienced by senior adults whose children have little contact with them. These aging people know they could become ill and die without once again seeing their children. Sometimes it happens. In these situations, pastors and other caregivers need to provide pastoral care and mobilize the congregation's and community's resources for emotional support for these senior adults.

Grandchildren. By this point in the discussion about children, the pastor or other caregiver will probably know whether the senior adults have grandchildren or great-grandchildren. If not, it is important to ask, "Do you have grandchildren or great-grandchildren?" (part V, G), because usually this is a key area of family life for senior adults. Being invited to respond to the question "How have they brought joy to your life?" (part V, H) will in most cases lead to an enjoyable conversation.

VI. Emergency Contact

Ask senior adults whom to contact for them in an emergency. It is imperative to record a telephone number, E-mail address (if available), and mailing address.

Helping Raymond to Share the Family Values

When I left Raymond's home, I drove to the church parking lot and quickly wrote my assessment and plan. I knew that I would be late for my next appointment, but I had learned from experience that if I try to rely on my memory and make the assessment and plan at the conclusion of all my visits I may forget something important. I called the church secretary on my cellular telephone and asked her to call the other senior adults on my afternoon home visitation schedule to inform them that I was behind schedule. This would assure them that I would be there.

Assessment and Plan

I. Professional Objectivity

- A. How do I feel about Raymond? I like Raymond. I wish that one of his daughters had notified me when he had a stroke so I could have offered pastoral care. I also feel sad for him that he still has so much grief work to do, nine years after his wife's death.
- B. Does he have life issues that are similar to mine that would make it difficult for me to be objective? I once experienced delayed grief because I was unable to attend an aunt's funeral. While that experience may help me to understand Raymond better, it could interfere with my objectivity.
- C. Do I have countertransference issues? If so, what are they? While my mother is not in need of nearly so much assistance as Raymond is, I too am an adult caregiver who drives almost four hours to help my mother. I need to be careful that I do not relate too closely with Raymond and his daughters.
- D. Does Raymond have transference issues? If so, what are they? He seemed to be very much aware that I am his pastor. I will need to make sure that he does not begin to view me as a fifth daughter.

II. Senior Adult's Agenda

- A. What does Raymond want?
    1. Spiritually: He wants to continue receiving communion. He also wants to prepare for death by telling his daughters about their grandparents.

2. Psychologically: He wants to be at peace before he dies.
3. Familially: He wants to leave a family legacy for his children, grandchildren, and potential great-grandchildren. He wants them to learn about his loving and faithful parents.
4. Socioeconomically: He expressed no needs.
5. Medically: He expressed no wants.

III. Pastor's or Other Caregiver's Assessment

A. Spiritual

1. Assessment: He needs to receive regularly scheduled home communion. He also needs to prepare for his inevitable death by telling his daughters about their grandparents.
2. Ways to foster growth: Tell him I will bring him home communion on a regular basis. Affirm his need to prepare for death by talking to his daughters about his parents. Ask him if he would like me to be present to help him talk to them.

B. Psychological

1. Assessment: While he needs to talk with his daughters about his parents, he also needs to work on his grief over his wife's death nine years ago.
2. Ways to foster growth: Encourage him to talk with his daughters. Give him permission to shed tears with his daughters. Help him understand that the tears would be sacred tears of love. Ask him if he would like to have me present when he talks with his daughters. This is the immediate assessment. However, in the near future, initiate a conversation about his wife's death and help him work on his grief.

C. Family

1. Assessment: He wants to leave his children, grandchildren, and potential great-grandchildren a family legacy of love, faith in God, and hard work. He wants them to know that the legacy began with his parents.
2. Ways to foster growth: Encourage him to talk with his daughters. Ask him if would like me to be present when he talks with them.

D. Socioeconomic

1. Assessment: He may benefit by increased social support.
2. Way to foster growth: I will ask him if he would like a lay visitor, and I will explain the Stephen Ministries program.

E. Medical
   1. Assessment: While he did not express a fear of falling, I sense that he is concerned about it in light of all the precautions he takes.
   2. Way to foster growth: Next time bring a brochure describing the local emergency-alert system, which he and his daughters may wish to consider.

IV. Plan for Responding to the Senior Adult's Needs
   A. What church resources are available to address Raymond's needs? The pastor (me) and the Stephen Ministries program.
      1. Who is available to contact them? I will provide follow-up pastoral care. After my next visit, if Raymond indicates that he would like a lay visitor, I will contact the program coordinator.
      2. When will contact be made? When appropriate.
      3. When will the plan be implemented? I have already scheduled another visit with Raymond next Wednesday afternoon.
      4. Date on which to provide for follow-up: The visit is already scheduled.
   B. What community resources are available to address Raymond's needs? I have brochures on the emergency-alert system in the trunk of my car. It is too early in our visitation to make assessments about community resources. Since his daughters care for him well, the priority now is to encourage him to talk about his parents with his daughters. At a future time, Raymond and his daughters may need information about community resources.
      1. Who is available to contact the resources? Not applicable now.
      2. When will the contact me made? Not applicable now.
      3. When will the plan be implemented? I'll bring the brochure next time.
      4. Date on which to provide for follow-up? Not applicable now.

V. Likely Consequences if I Elect to Do Less or More than Expected or Needed
   A. Spiritual consequences: Raymond may die regretting that he did not talk to his daughters about their family legacy.
   B. Psychological consequences: He may remain distressed. Yet he has the option of not talking to his daughters.

C. Family consequences: The articulated family legacy may not be passed on.
D. Socioeconomic consequences: He may remain lonelier than necessary.
E. Medical consequences: None now.

When I returned to Raymond's home on the following Wednesday, he was looking out the window awaiting my arrival. He welcomed me warmly. As we started talking, I briefly reviewed with him what we had discussed in our previous visit. I could tell immediately that he wanted to continue the conversation. He became tearful as we talked about his loving relationship with his daughters. When I saw his tears, I said, "Raymond, your tears are sacred tears of love for your daughters." I was surprised at his willingness to talk about tears. As he said that he is embarrassed because he cries so easily now, I told him crying is also one of the side effects of a stroke. He was both surprised and relieved to learn this. We further discussed what his parents were like and what he wanted to tell his daughters about them. After I offered to be with him when he talked to his daughters, he said, "You would? That would help because we are all going to be crying." I obtained the names and telephone numbers of his daughters. That evening after I called one of them, she said she would call me the next day (after she had talked to her sisters) with some possible dates we could all get together.

CHAPTER 5

Economic and Societal Influences on Aging

Fred: Losing Financial Self-Sufficiency

As I went to visit Fred (a widower of 85) on my regular monthly visit to bring Holy Communion, I had no idea on entering his home how surprised I would feel before I left. I had visited Fred monthly for ten months. His deep appreciation for Holy Communion was always reflected in his tearful eyes. He told me that his tears expressed his gratitude for all that God had done for him in sending Jesus to die for his sins and for the peace God gives him now and will more fully give him in heaven.

Fred is on my visitation schedule because he is permanently homebound. Debilitating arthritis prevents him from leaving his house, except occasionally to get a haircut (he uses senior citizen transportation to take him to the barbershop). To assist him with activities of daily life Fred has a housekeeper who cleans his house twice a month, a person who mows his lawn in the summer and shovels his snow in the winter, and a daughter who drives 200 miles round-trip to do his laundry weekly. Each time I visit Fred, his middle-class house is well kept and he is well groomed. Fred previously told me that he is content with being homebound because in the course of each day he relives memories of his previous employment years and his family life.

During this visit he was eager once again to hear what was happening at the church. In previous visits we had discussed why our congregation is important to him, which committees he had served on, which worship leadership roles he had held, and the meaning each leadership role had for him. In our conversation today, however, he focused on the finances of the church and wondered if the church bills were being paid.

This was a new area of conversation for us. I told him that the church was doing fairly well this summer compared to other summers and that while we were $3,000 short, this shortage was less than in previous years. Looking troubled, Fred said, "I feel so guilty."

"Fred, what do you feel guilty about?" I asked.

"I feel so guilty because I can't help pay the bills. All I have to live on is my Social Security, and I receive the smallest amount they give," he blurted out with a deep sigh. As we discussed this subject, Fred said, "You know, I've never told you this before, but at this time [the end] of the month, I have a hard time making it." He paused and slowly continued: "I have to pay my cleaning person and the person who shovels the snow. Plus my heating bill is very high because I need my house to be warm due to my arthritis. Oh, I probably shouldn't tell you all this. I guess I'm having a blue day." Fred and I discussed his beliefs about financial stewardship, his frustration with living on a fixed income, the difference between "being" and "doing" or "producing" as a way of living in God's unconditional love, and his feelings of discouragement.

Near the end of our visit, considering all that Fred had newly disclosed to me and our relationship of ten months, I asked directly, "Fred, do you have enough food to eat?" After he hung his head and paused, he slowly and sadly said, "Right now the only food I have in the house is one pint of milk and four slices of bread, until I get my Social Security check in three days." Fred also told me that he was too embarrassed to tell his daughter about his situation and that he did not want me to tell her either.

Socioeconomic Issues

The areas in the socioeconomic component are not an exhaustive list of sociological and economic issues in people's lives. They are socioeconomic issues that I have found in my ministry with senior adults to be important in their aging process. Often the issues are directly related to senior adults' relationships with God and influence how they perceive or fail to perceive meaning in life. Sometimes the pastor or other caregiver may need to help find assistance for these problems. This component guides conversation and assists the caregiver to assess critical socioeconomic needs and to plan how to address them.

I. Employment

As I hear senior adults share their employment history (Part I, A), whenever possible I connect the discussion with our previous conversations about faith. For example, I help them to explore the meaning employment had during their working years. I might say to a retired factory worker, "The work you did in making quality soup contributed to customers' good nutrition so they could live healthy lives." Or I may say to a retired lawyer, "The work you did as an active Christian in helping people was a way of promoting God's justice and equality in the world." In offering such comments, I attempt to help retirees recognize the meaning of their past employment and to affirm the important (and sometimes sacrificial) difference they made in God's creation.

Not all employment experiences are positive, however (part I, E). Retired seniors may need to discuss unresolved employment issues. They may still have unresolved guilt feelings for not attending Sunday worship regularly when an employer required them to work on Sunday, for their acquiescence with an employer's order to perform unethical duties, or for stealing items from the workplace as a way to survive on low wages. They may also feel unresolved resentment toward an employer who treated them unfairly. Retired people may need to discuss unresolved anger, especially if they experienced harassment or discrimination in the workplace. These senior adults may have thought they had no recourse to the ill treatment because jobs were difficult to find and they needed the income. In these and related situations, I help senior adults to articulate the unresolved issues, to identify how God gave them courage and strength to survive the past experiences, and to believe that God will continue to provide courage and strength for the challenges of aging.

II. Retirement

Retirement can be a great blessing or a great challenge for senior adults (part II, B). For those who were able to plan for their retirement in advance and retire at a specific time with good health and positive goals, retirement can be a pleasure. For others, forced into retirement by downsizing or poor health (with no opportunity to formulate goals and plans for retirement), it can be a depressing experience.

Finances greatly affect one's retirement (part II, C). For senior adults of financial means, retirement can mean new opportunities and experiences. But for those with less money, life can be difficult, lonely, and depressing. Fred, a self-employed laborer before his retirement, did not receive a pension, and his Social Security check was so inadequate that he could not afford to buy food at the end of the month, let alone pursue any outside interests.

The caregiver's approach to pastoral care with retirees is, of course, based on the individual's reaction to retirement. It is easy to rejoice and give thanks for God's goodness with older people for whom retirement is positive. It is a greater challenge to help depressed retirees to experience meaning and hope. Their experience may be similar to that of the psalmist who wrote, "[M]y eyes are tired from so much crying; I am completely worn out. I am exhausted by sorrow, and weeping has shortened my life. I am weak from all my troubles; even my bones are wasting away" (Ps. 31:9-10, TEV). The caregiver may need to respond with words of wisdom in the mode of Paul Tillich: "The courage to be is rooted in the God who appears when God has appeared in the anxiety of doubt."[1] The caregiver's assessment and plan help these senior adults to recognize their value to God and others around them, as well as to find meaning in their retirement.

III. Financial

It may be necessary for the pastor or other caregiver to raise the issue of finances (part III, A). Sometimes this must be done immediately, as when the caregiver makes an initial home visit and observes unmistakable poverty. At other times this is done only after a trust relationship has developed, as when senior adults who previously seemed outwardly capable of providing for the needs of daily life now drop hints about a critical life situation. This was the case with Fred when I directly inquired, "Fred, do you have enough food to eat?" (part III, B, C).

Financial stress occurs for some senior adults because their income after retirement is lower than during their working years, and their expenses increase, especially their medical bills, Medicare supplemental insurance premiums, medication costs not covered by insurance, fees for home-health-care workers, property taxes, and home-upkeep expenses. Unfortunately, senior adults may attempt to compensate for these expenses by reducing the amount of money they spend for food and medication, to the detriment of their overall health.

As the caregiver assesses financial need, she or he needs to develop a plan for the most appropriate way to address the need. Possibilities include making senior adults' families aware of the financial need, suggesting professional daily money management for senior adults who become confused or overanxious when dealing with finances, providing food through a community or congregational food shelf and the pastor's discretionary fund, and contacting county social service agencies. The intent is not for the caregiver to become a social worker but for the caregiver to respond to senior adults' financial needs.

Senior adults' financial situations may or may not directly influence their experience of God and the church, or affect their abilities to experience meaning in life. When aging people have adequate incomes to provide for basic needs of life, their experience of God may be positive. On the other hand, when they have inadequate incomes and are unable to meet their daily needs in a healthy way, they may ask, as Erma did, "Pastor, what did I do wrong in my life to warrant my financial problems?" The answer may be, "You did nothing wrong. You are a victim of the injustice in our world, as some people have more opportunities earlier in life to save for retirement than other people do. I, however, want you to know that God loves you, will continue to give you strength to meet your challenges, and wants you to live a meaningful life. Now, let's talk about how God does this for you."

IV. Time

Responses to the question, "How do you spend your days and evenings?" (part I, A) give the caregiver an indication of whether senior adults use time in meaningful ways (for example, reading, hobbies), experience time as meaningless (for example, sitting, staring, or lamenting), or relish time as a peaceful opportunity for spiritual growth (for example, praying or working on the Spiritual Journey Exercise for Individuals).

Caregivers have the opportunity to go beyond the scope of this simple question about time ("How do you spend your days and evenings?) and help senior adults realize that time can be spiritually meaningful if they relate daily life to faith. For example, I said to Julian, "When you watch television, listen to the radio, or read the newspaper and learn about problems in the world, if you pray about the situations and the people affected by them, these negative situations will take on a meaningful spiritual dimension." After Georgia asked how she could use her time at home to grow in faith, I said, "Why don' you try the Spiritual Journey Exercise for Individuals [appendix A]? Take your time going through it. As you do so, you will grow in faith."

While the caregiver develops assessments and plans for how to bring deeper spiritual meaning to senior adults' experiences of time, ultimately it is the individual's choice whether or not to engage in such a process.

V. Socialization

Ask senior adults, "How do you socialize with others?" (part V, A) to assess whether they lack social contact. Senior adults who have little or no contact with people may feel abandoned by society and by God, especially as they experience limitations related to aging. Their feelings may reflect those of the psalmist who wrote, "Everyone has forgotten me, as though I were dead; I am like something thrown away" (Ps. 31:12, TEV).

Senior adults may lack socialization for many reasons. Some may have been loners or introverts all their lives. Their inability or unwillingness now to initiate relationships is a consistent life pattern. Other senior adults have health conditions that make them want to stay home, even when they live alone. Some who raised their children to be independent and successful may not receive frequent visits from those children. Other aging people prefer being home by themselves, where they feel more secure. Yet others are isolated because they cannot financially afford to socialize with their friends. Nursing home residents also may be socially isolated, except for the limited professional social support from health care providers.

When I sense that senior adults are socially isolated, I find it helpful to ask, "How many times during the past week did you talk with a friend or family member?" (part V, B). While the pastor or other caregiver cannot be expected through home visitation to fill the socialization role for senior adults, he or she can enlist others to assist in addressing this need. The assessment and plan can include matching senior adults with the congregation's lay home visitation program, providing rides (through volunteer drivers) to church events, and contacting community senior citizen centers and social service agencies that have programs to serve the socialization needs of senior citizens.

Frequently as senior adults have more contact with people, they also begin to experience a higher level of self-worth and a closer relationship with God.

VI. Living Situation

Part VI is included in the socioeconomic component merely as an area of observation for caregivers. Because the living situations of senior adults may change during the course of long-term visitation, I find it helpful to note when the changes occur, as well as the reason for the changes (if I know the reason). Not only does it help me to stay current with their lives, but it may also affect how I provide pastoral services for them.

VII. Education

Knowledge of senior adults' educational backgrounds can assist the caregiver to develop insights into aging people's abilities to participate meaningfully in pastoral conversation, especially within the scope of the comprehensive Parish Spiritual Assessment Tool. Sometimes the level of education completed affects one's ability both to think through problems methodically and to articulate one's thoughts. Aging people's educational levels may also affect their self-images, especially if they base part of their self-worth upon their education. If senior adults attended college, the choice of school may also give an indication of their faith (Did they attend a church-related college?) and interests (What was their college major?). At the same time, however, pastors and other caregivers know that the amount of education which a person has completed is not necessarily indicative of the depth and meaning of faith.

VIII. Societal Limitation Factors

Even though the societal limitation factors in Part VIII overlap slightly with other categories (for example, medical), these factors often impinge significantly on senior adults' life satisfaction by limiting their current opportunities in similar ways in which their opportunities were limited in earlier years (part VIII, A). The mere identification of these factors can reassure and enlighten senior adults. As they learn that factors in society which are beyond their control cause limitations for them, they are less likely to blame themselves for how the factors continue to influence their lives.

People in authority. Senior adults may encounter authorities in the medical community who have their own agenda and ignore senior adults' insights into their own medical conditions. Even though senior adults may articulate their symptoms well, sometimes medical professionals minimize the symptoms.

Pastors and lay leaders also sometimes minimize the needs of senior adults. They may fail to consider how language affects senior adults. For example, even though the largest percentage of Sunday worshippers may be senior adults, the lay and pastoral leadership in congregations may publicly state that the future of the congregation is found only in young families. This type of thinking devalues the importance of the congregation's senior adult membership. Language and congregational decisions need to be congruent so that public statements about the value of senior adults are followed up with actions. For example, actions such as installing an elevator, increasing the number of parking spaces for the disabled, putting senior adults on the congregation's governing body and using them as worship assistants, continuing to hold traditional liturgical services along with contemporary services, providing large-print bulletins and newsletters, and making visitation of homebound elderly a priority will indicate to senior adults that their congregation values them.

Legal professionals and politicians sometimes fail to advocate for the needs of senior adults. Decisions made by these people in authority can reduce both the quality of life and life satisfaction for senior adults. Seniors' lives are adversely affected by state and federal budget cuts in human services, moratoriums on the building of nursing homes, restrictions on wages paid to nursing home employees, failure to include medications in Medicare benefits for the homebound, and reductions in or elimination of cost-of-living increases in monthly Social Security checks.

These attitudes of people in authority fail to recognize senior adults' God-given goodness, value, and identity. The caregiver who makes an assessment that "people in authority ignore the senior adult's ability to assess personal needs" may need to develop a pastoral plan either to become the senior adult's personal advocate or to find someone else who will. The caregiver needs to bring such concerns to the senior advisory committee, which may decide to mobilize the congregation to advocate politically for senior adults. This can be done through letter writing campaigns in which the senior advisory committee can provide the congregation with sample letters advocating for specific needs of senior adults.

Gender stereotypes. Stereotypical gender roles and attitudes may be quite prevalent among this generation. Just as these stereotypes have limited the opportunities for senior adults in the past, they may continue to have a residual effect in the present, even though gender attitudes continue to change. Gender stereotypes can reduce life satisfaction in both women and men. For example, an older woman may have believed in her younger years that culture mandated that she marry, have children, serve as caretaker for her husband and children, sacrifice herself for others, never ask for help, always be strong for others, and maintain control of her life for the sake of her family. Now in her later years, she may experience low self-worth as she compares the subservient role which she accepted in earlier life with the more assertive role assumed by younger professional women in today's culture. Even though she is aware of the changing role of women, this elderly woman may still believe that it would be inappropriate for her (at this stage in life) to become assertive in getting her needs met.

Aging men also face gender stereotypes. For example, Raoul said, "In my day, a man didn't change jobs just because he was unhappy at his place of employment. A man was the only breadwinner in the family. Now I wish I had changed jobs, but I just didn't have the courage. If I had changed jobs, I would have found one where I had more time at home with my children. Since I put in such long hours at work, my wife raised the kids by herself. I never got to know my children, and they didn't get to know me. I really missed out!" Raoul is aware that stereotypical gender roles continue to affect him today. He still hesitates to initiate contact with his children, both because he has had no experience doing so, and because he is unsure what to say to them.

The caregiver who assesses that a senior adult continues to be limited by stereotypical gender roles may need to develop a plan that affirms the senior adult's God-given value and that encourages and empowers him or her to become assertive in getting needs met. This may mean that the over-65 adult relearns how to function in contemporary society so that she or he can lead a more satisfying life.

Medical reimbursement. Another societal limitation that may reduce life satisfaction in senior adults is their inability to pay for adequate medical care. Senior adults who are required to reduce the quality of their post-retirement medical care because they cannot afford to purchase Medicare supplement insurance may be unable to obtain medical care from physicians who do not accept Medicare payment for services. This often also means that senior adults cannot receive care from medical specialists. When this is my assessment, my pastoral plan includes contacting the county social service agency to explore options for medical assistance and reminding senior adults about their value to God, Jesus' love for them, and their congregation's love. This is another societal limitation that constantly needs to be brought to the attention of lawmakers, so that Medicare laws can be changed.

Transportation problems. Senior adults who no longer drive, who lack the mobility to use public transportation, who live where there is no public transportation, or who cannot afford public transportation, usually experience reduced life satisfaction and quality of life. When this is the assessment, the caregiver's plan may include becoming involved in a civic process to develop adequate community transportation for senior adults, enlisting the services of church volunteers to serve as drivers or travel companions for senior adults, and engaging senior adults in conversation about dealing spiritually with the grief of losing independence.

The pastor or other caregiver sometimes becomes involved in the difficult decision of whether a senior adult is still capable of driving safely. Concerned people, such as congregational members, family members, or other citizens, may advise the caregiver that a specific senior member who still drives is a danger to herself or himself, as well as to passengers and other motorists. The unsafe driver may suffer from dementia, visual impairment, hearing loss, or arthritic feet or hands. Sometimes the matter of driving privileges becomes an issue of genuine concern in the congregation. Members may be afraid to ride with the person or may worry that she or he will get lost while driving. When I assess that the member is an unsafe driver, my plan includes enlisting the assistance of the family (if there is a family) to discuss the situation with the older adult. The unpleasant solutions may include asking the family physician to tell the elderly patient that it is now time to quit driving for medical reasons; asking law-enforcement officials to prohibit the senior adult from driving by lawfully withdrawing driving privileges; or removing the car keys or disabling the vehicle. My plan also includes offering pastoral care to the senior adult whose driving privileges have been revoked, to the family, and to the concerned church members.

Stereotypes about aging. Society's view of the aged is, unfortunately, often negative. When I assess that senior adults suffer emotionally or spiritually from society's negative view of aging, I have a wonderful opportunity to develop a pastoral plan to counteract that view by citing passages from the Bible. For example, from the Old Testament Creation story (Gen. 1), I remind senior adults that they are created in God's image and that God proclaims them to be "very good." From the Holiness Code (Lev. 19:32) and the Fourth Commandment (Exod. 20:12), I counteract society's negative view by telling senior adults that God commands society to honor aged people. Through references to ancient social systems (for example Deut. 21:1-9, Num. 11:16-17), I remind senior adults that just as the elders of Israel used their lifelong experiences to help other people make decisions, so can the senior adults of today. From Proverbs (Prov. 1:8-9; 6:20-22; 23:22-25), I affirm senior adults' wisdom and their value to the world.

I point out that the story of Jesus in the New Testament begins with an aging couple (Anna and Simeon) who proclaim God's redemptive purposes through the birth of Jesus (Luke 2:25-38). I also share with senior adults Jesus' teachings that proclaim the importance of "being," as contrasted with "producing" (Matt. 6:25-26), and Jesus' command that people love neighbors of all ages, including the aging (Matt. 22:37-40). I also share Jesus' words of comfort and compassion for senior adults (Matt. 5:1-12, 11:28), and his promise of salvation for them (John 3:16). As this pastoral plan attempts to counteract society's negative view of the aged, it also offers senior adults deeper spiritual meaning for life. I exhort senior adults to make these passages, as well as their baptismal covenant, the basis of their value and identity.

Easing Fred's Financial Needs

When I left Fred's home, I drove part way around the block so he would not see me sitting in my car as I worked on my laptop computer for the assessment and plan. If he saw me, he might think our visit was not concluded.

Assessment and Plan Component

Part I. Professional Objectivity.

A. How do I feel about Fred? I like Fred and love him as a child of God. Today I also feel sad about his financial situation.

B. Does he have life issues that are similar to mine that would make it difficult for me to be objective? No, unless my lifelong passion to feed the hungry would lead me to empathize even more deeply with Fred.

C. Do I have countertransference issues? I may associate Fred with the hungry people I see on the television news broadcasts and in the print media.

D. Does Fred have transference issues? He may or may not view me as his daughter.

Part II. Senior Adult's Agenda

A. What does Fred want?
  1. Spiritually: Fred wants to be able to contribute financially to his congregation.
  2. Psychologically: Fred may want help to deal with his depression.
  3. Familially: Fred wants to keep his socioeconomic situation confidential so that his daughter does not become aware of it.
  4. Socioeconomically: Fred wants to be financially independent.
  5. Medically: Fred expressed no wants or needs today.

Part III. Pastor or Other Caregiver's Assessment

A. Spiritual
  1. Assessment: Fred feels guilty because he cannot afford to contribute financially to the church.
  2. Way to foster growth: Next time continue to discuss the meaning and importance of "being" and God's unconditional love.

B. Psychological
  1. Assessment: Fred is depressed because of his limited financial resources.
  2. Way to foster growth: Next time continue to discuss the meaning and importance of "being" and God's unconditional love.

C. Family
  1. Assessment: Although Fred's daughter visits him weekly and does his laundry, he does not want to share his financial situation with her.
  2. Way to foster growth: Next time (if appropriate) gently seek Fred's permission to contact his daughter.

D. Socioeconomic
   1. Assessment: Fred needs food.
   2. Way to foster growth: Obtain food for Fred.
E. Medical
   1. Assessment: Fred expressed no needs; however, if he does not obtain food, he will deteriorate medically.
   2. Way to foster growth: Obtain food for Fred.

Part IV. Plan for Responding to the Senior Adult's Needs
A. What church resources are available to address Fred's needs? The food shelf.
   1. Who is available to contact the food shelf coordinator? The pastor (in order to keep it confidential).
   2. When will the contact be made? Immediately.
   3. When will the plan be implemented? Today.
   4. Date on which to provide for follow-up: Since Fred will receive food today and his Social Security check will arrive in three days, I can wait until my next visit with Fred to monitor his situation further.
B. What community resources are available to address Fred's needs? The county social service department can evaluate whether Fred qualifies for financial assistance with subsidized meals-on-wheels, housekeeping services, and heating assistance. The senior citizen center might be able to provide free snow shoveling and lawn mowing through its volunteer chore-service program.
   1. Who is available to contact the resources? The pastor (in order to keep it confidential).
   2. When will the contacts me made? Today.
   3. When will the plan be implemented? The county social service department and senior citizen center will need time to evaluate Fred's needs and initiate their procedures.
   4. Date on which to provide for follow-up? Telephone the community resource people in one week. In the meantime Fred has the food from the church, and he will receive his Social Security check in a few days so that he will be able to purchase food. If the response is unfavorable from the social service department, call or visit Fred again, bring him more food if he needs it, and ask his permission to contact his daughter.

Part V. Likely Consequences if the Pastor or Other Caregiver Elects to Do Less or More than Expected or Needed.

A. Spiritual consequences: If I do not follow through with Fred about the meaning and importance of "being" and God's unconditional love, Fred may not experience the peace of God.

B. Psychological consequences: If I do not set in motion a process for Fred to receive food and possibly other services, he may remain depressed because of his inability to advocate for himself.

C. Family consequences: If I do not contact Fred's daughter, she will have no opportunity to provide food for her father. However, if I do not obtain Fred's permission to contact her and I do so anyway, I will go against Fred's specific request and I will lose his trust. I need to allow Fred to keep his dignity by being able to provide for himself, preferably by receiving county assistance. If he is unable to obtain such assistance, I will discuss with him the need for us to involve his daughter.

D. Socioeconomic consequences: If I do not obtain food for Fred, he will go hungry. If I provide food more often than he needs assistance, he may lose his dignity because he wants to be as self-sufficient and independent as possible.

E. Medical consequences: If I do not follow through with obtaining food for Fred, his medical condition will deteriorate.

Fred's socioeconomic situation resolved positively. Our congregational food shelf provided more than enough food for him until his next Social Security check would arrive and he could purchase food for himself. The county social service department determined that Fred was eligible for subsidized meals-on-wheels. This decision alleviated his need to struggle in the kitchen preparing meals and provided him with an additional social contact per day from the delivery person. The social service department also determined that Fred was eligible for heating assistance. The senior citizen center found a volunteer who began to shovel Fred's snow. The senior citizen center also offered to find a volunteer to mow Fred's lawn next summer. Through the course of pastoral visitation, we further discussed his financial situation. I was able to encourage Fred to share his financial needs with his daughter, who completely and lovingly took over monitoring and responding to Fred's financial needs. I then continued my role as Fred's parish pastor and informally continued to make use of my Parish Spiritual Assessment Tool with him, as he chose to participate.

CHAPTER 6

A Medical Overview

Harris: Relief for the Helpless

In his younger years, 92-year-old Harris had been energetic and hard-working. As a self-employed house painter, he had a reputation for taking pride in his work and wanting to please his clients. Behind closed doors with his wife and two sons, however, he took on a different personality. Except for his unpredictable outbursts of anger, he took no interest in his family. His wife and sons became frustrated when people in the community talked about what a "great guy" he was because they never saw that person. Nonetheless, the family attended worship together, and Harris sometimes served as a substitute usher.

Within a three-year span Harris's life changed dramatically. His older son joined the army the day after high school graduation. His younger son graduated from high school a year later and chose to move 500 miles away to attend college. The following year Harris's wife died of a massive stroke. While Harris continued to work as a painter, he became a recluse during his off hours.

When he retired at age 76, he had no friends. He had stopped attending church except at Christmas and Easter (when he could become lost in the crowds). His older son never called, and the younger son telephoned only a few times a year. As his health deteriorated, Harris could no longer see to read. He suffered from intermittent incontinence, developed pain in his shoulders and arms from his years as a painter, and struggled with arthritic hands. He was prone to falls–one leg was weaker than the other as a result of standing unevenly on ladders. Occasionally he was incapacitated by severe headaches, and he frequently had insomnia. He learned to deal with his multiple challenges by having groceries and medications delivered to his home (they were left at the door), receiving meals-on-wheels (they were also left at the door), relying on volunteers from the senior citizen center to mow his lawn and shovel his sidewalk (they were never allowed in his house), and employing a housekeeper who cleaned his home twice a month. His only social contacts were his housekeeper, his brief phone conversations when placing an order, and the people he saw on his large-screen television or heard on the radio.

I had no knowledge of Harris until one Sunday in church when I overheard a conversation between two senior adult ushers. One said to the other, "I wonder whatever happened to Harris." The next day I searched for Harris's name in our office computer. I discovered that while Harris was officially a member, no one in the office knew anything about him. Even though I immediately telephoned him, it took four calls before Harris trusted me enough to allow me to come to his house and bring him communion.

Harris and I developed a close relationship during the next nine months. It was immediately evident that he had had no extended conversations with anyone for years. His agenda was to use me as a sounding board for his age-related medical problems. He had not talked with anyone because he had such a backlog of woes to discuss. Despite multiple physical challenges, the measures that he had taken to deal with them seemed adequate to respond to his daily needs. As I engaged him in discussions about his faith, his favorite topics to talk about (only briefly, of course) were the importance of prayer and Holy Communion. He had no interest in further discussions about his religious background. Overall, Harris's demeanor was quiet, and he seemed to enjoy living as a hermit. When I asked if he would like a lay visitor, he bluntly said, "No! I won't let anyone else in my house!"

Then the infamous day arrived. I immediately knew Harris needed help. I arrived just after the meals-on-wheels delivery person brought him lunch. Harris could not differentiate between the chicken and the bones. When he tried to pour milk, he missed the glass. Besides the packages of moldy food on his kitchen table, loose pills were strewn about–red pills, white pills, green pills, and blue pills all mixed together. Some pills had fallen to the floor. The empty back burner of the stove was red-hot. Water was accumulating on the kitchen floor from the overflowing kitchen sink, piled high with dirty dishes in dirty water. It was hot in the house because Harris could not see to read the numbers on the thermostat.

As Harris slowly spoke, I immediately realized that his speech was slurred. This was the first time he had spoken with slurred speech since I had met him. All he could say was, "Could you take this chicken meat off the bone for me? I'm just not having a good day." Harris's life now was out of control. He was no longer safe in his home.

Medical Issues

While this medical component is not a tool for gathering comprehensive medical information, it provides an overview of the medical issues that caregivers need to be aware of during visitation with senior adults. Some parts of the component, such as senior adults' "reasons for being homebound," can be completed by observation, while other parts, such as "health status," may need to be discussed. By having a blueprint of what to look for, the caregiver can more easily develop medical assessments and plans. Sometimes senior adults are fully capable of assessing their own health conditions and seeking medical care for themselves. At other times they may need either referrals or immediate intervention so they do not become unsafe living alone because of health conditions.

Some senior adults who capably manage their own health care still may be significantly concerned about their medical situation and wish to discuss it during visitation. I find that one effective way to avoid being tempted to focus primarily on medical problems is to apply relevant parts of the Parish Spiritual Assessment Tool to the situation that they experience. For example:

- Using the spiritual component, I may engage in a discussion about how senior adults cope with illness (part VIII, H), whether they feel their current problem may lead to death (part IX), and how they make medical decisions (part X).
- Using the psychological component, I may engage in a discussion about depression (part IV) with those who seem discouraged about their medical condition.
- Using the family component, I may inquire if they would like to contact relatives who may be able to help them (part VI) get in touch with their medical care providers.
- Using the socioeconomic component, I may engage senior adults in discussions about how they spend their time (part IV) and socialize (part V) when they are ill, or whether they are considering a change in

living arrangements (part VI) that would provide them with more medical care.

In visitation with senior adults who are unable to monitor their own health needs, who have no family, or who have an unsupportive family, my observations and assessments may lead me to decide that I need to address the medical situation directly. I may need to refer them to medical professionals. Sometimes I research their medical problem on the Internet, using credible Web sites.

Record-keeping, including regularly updating senior adults' medical status, is fundamental to providing good pastoral care. When the older adult is medically stable, the caregiver needs to record only a brief statement. Gradual changes can be briefly noted. When more significant changes occur, more complete record-keeping can be useful. Reviewing notes before a visit helps me to remember medical changes in senior adults' lives, so that instead of having to take visiting time for a review of their past medical history, the session can be used to talk about what their medical changes and conditions mean to them.

I. Reasons for Being Homebound

Temporarily homebound. I find that it is helpful when placing senior adults on my home visitation list to ascertain whether they are temporarily or permanently homebound. I usually make this determination from observations during the initial visit. Only infrequently do I find it necessary to ask, "What are your reasons for being homebound?" I also keep a separate list of temporarily homebound senior adults so that they remain part of my visitation schedule as long as needed. Unless I intentionally schedule visits with temporarily homebound persons, I might visit them once and think that is sufficient. Sometimes people can be temporarily homebound for months at a time.

Senior adults temporarily homebound because of illness, accident, or convalescence after hospitalization may realistically anticipate that they will either return to their previous level of activity or at least return to a level close to it. Their physicians may, in fact, give them approximate timelines. Such prognoses, of course, will frequently fill them with hope during this temporary change in lifestyle. They also may be encouraged by family and friends to look forward to a positive future. On the other hand, when temporarily homebound senior adults are discouraged by their status, the caregiver's assessment and plan may include finding people from the congregation and community to provide additional visitation and support for them.

Spouses who provide in-home care for their invalid partners are another category of the temporarily homebound. Frequently their status is unrecognized by others. The invalid's partner provides 24-hour-a-day care. The challenge for pastors or other caregivers is to recognize that both spouses have become homebound, one permanently and one temporarily. Frequently when people visit such a couple, they will offer their primary support to the invalid and fail to realize that the lifestyle of the caregiver spouse has also changed radically.

As the pastor or other caregiver visits such a couple, it may be helpful to keep in mind some dynamics that the caregiver spouse might experience. She may find it necessary to give up church attendance, participation in community organizations or clubs, and other activities that previously provided meaning and enjoyment in life. As a result she may have mixed feelings about being homebound because of her husband's medical situation.

While a caregiver husband may, on the one hand, find satisfaction in fulfilling his marital vows to care for his wife in sickness and in health, on the other hand he may become angry and depressed as he begins to reach the end of his own physical or emotional energy. He may be unable to envision any improvement in the situation or any positive options for the future.

The temporary nature of a caregiver's homebound status sometimes ends when it becomes necessary to admit the invalid partner to a nursing home or when the partner dies at home. It may take years, however, for the caregiver to make the decision to admit the invalid spouse to a nursing home. A pastor visiting the homebound couple needs to offer support to both spouses, develop assessments and plans for both, and keep separate notes on each person so that ministry can be offered to both individuals.

Weather conditions can also cause senior adults to be temporarily homebound. Heat and high humidity may limit seniors prone to respiratory distress to remaining at home where they have air conditioning or can sit in front of a fan. If the church sanctuary is not air-conditioned, they will be unable to attend worship during the hot months of the year. Cold winter temperatures also can make it impossible for the aging to attend worship. Some may stay at home because inhaling cold air creates respiratory problems for them. Others may try to remain in their homes all winter to avoid falling on snow or ice and possibly breaking a bone. Those who drive may choose to become homebound in winter so they do not have to worry about accidents on icy roads or the car engine stalling and leaving them stranded. Still others may have a lowered immune system that leaves them susceptible to contracting winter illnesses. Some patients even refrain from scheduling winter medical appointments to avoid the large number of sick people in the waiting areas of medical offices.

Some people are homebound only at specific times of day. For example, some senior adults take medications that make them dizzy in the morning, so they need to stay home until afternoon. Arthritic conditions may make it hard to accomplish morning personal chores (such as dressing, eating, bathing, and walking). Yet as the day progresses, the arthritic elder is able to be more active. Medications used to address gastrointestinal or urinary problems may necessitate that the patient remain close to the bathroom in the morning. Patients on kidney dialysis may have only limited energy after the day's dialysis. They may also be too tired on the following days to be active. Dressing changes on wounds that need to be done at certain times of the day or week may restrict when older adults can leave home. The same may be true for those who have home physical therapy or respiratory treatments. Diabetics who prefer giving themselves insulin injections at home will restrict their outside activity to the times between injections. For those whose visual acuity is reduced after dark, going out in the evening for church activities may be impossible. The fear of becoming a crime victim may restrict some seniors from leaving home.

Sometimes this type of temporary homebound status is misunderstood by pastors or other caregivers. They may question why they are requested to bring home communion to members who are able to schedule appointments with hair stylists or doctors, go out to eat, or even go shopping. Yet as caregivers become aware of the complexity of this time-sensitive homebound status, they will realize that older people in these situations are truly unable to attend Sunday morning worship and may genuinely need and cherish pastoral visitation and home communion. The caregivers will also recognize that being able to go out (even in a limited way) is a blessing for senior adults because it positively affects their self-esteem, sense of independence, and physical health.

Permanently homebound. Physical limitations, psychological distress, lack of transportation, or a combination of these factors may be the most frequent reasons that senior adults become permanently homebound. The list of possible health conditions in part II (Health status) will be helpful for the pastor or other caregiver in identifying the multiple factors that affect senior adults.

Physical limitations are most often caused by illness, disease, accident, or the aging process. While senior adults are faced with some of the same medical challenges as younger people, the aging are more prone to becoming permanently homebound because these conditions may be accompanied by visual or auditory impairment with no prognosis for improvement, incontinence with no available treatment, advanced arthritis, osteoporosis (which increases the likelihood of broken bones from falls), chronic pain, or chronic fatigue. As the number of medical problems increases, so does the tendency to become permanently homebound. Accompanying these limitations often is an increased level of frustration, especially when one first becomes permanently homebound.

Psychological stress may be another reason for which aging people become permanently homebound. Unresolved grief related to deaths of loved ones, loneliness, or depression may discourage senior adults from going out in public. The Parish Spiritual Assessment Tool is helpful in visiting with people who are grieving, lonely, or depressed. The discussion questions both provide a guide for pastoral conversation and assist troubled senior adults to find meaning in life and rediscover their sources of inner strength.

In visits with senior adults who experience dementia, Alzheimer's disease, or certain kinds of severe mental illness, a different strategy is often needed. It is more helpful to acknowledge their feelings and to affirm them as worthwhile and loved people of God, rather than to talk in details and attempt to get them to develop insights that they are incapable of making at this limited cognitive level. Also, in this situation, if the pastor or other caregiver reads a Bible passage to them, it is important to select a reading that focuses on the basic theme of God's love, rather than on the human creature's sinful condition. This is true because often such individuals will fixate on words. It is more pastoral to leave them fixated on the love of God than on their sinful condition.

Some homebound senior adults may pose a challenge for home visitation because they are timid. Obtaining a "yes" or "no" answer may be difficult, and longer discussions may be impossible. Sometimes, there are no family members to consult for help in learning what the senior adult may find meaningful to talk about. These visits can be awkward for both the aging person and the caregiver. Sometimes the senior adult's only agenda with the visitor is to receive communion. While this may be frustrating for the pastor who does not want to be thought of as a "wafer dropper," the senior adult's agenda needs to be respected.

Senior adults sometimes become permanently homebound because they lack transportation. Some who never learned to drive may become homebound when their spouse, who did all the driving, dies. Others may have quit driving because of visual or auditory impairment, weakness in arms or legs, fear of mechanical trouble on the road, expenses of car upkeep and insurance, or a history of driving accidents. Some live in small towns that have no buses or cabs. Still others may have had family members or law enforcement personnel tell them they can no longer drive because they are a hazard to themselves and others on the road. When aging people lack the financial resources to take taxis, or when they are afraid of taking taxis or buses, they become permanently homebound, especially if they also have no friends who drive and could offer them a ride. The assessment and plan for ministering to them may include finding volunteer drivers from the congregation or community who can give them an occasional ride.

II. Health Status

Part II (Health status) assists the pastor or other caregiver to develop an understanding of senior adults' health conditions, to discuss the meaning of those conditions with them, to help them (when necessary) learn how to obtain home health care so that they can remain in their own homes longer, and to make pastoral observations apart from the seniors' articulated descriptions of their health conditions.

Health over the past two years. When I ask, "How would you describe your health over the past year or two?" (part II, A), my purpose is to develop a picture of the changing nature of senior adults' health conditions. The fact that I am visiting them tells me that they have experienced a change; otherwise I would not be there. Yet the picture of their health is more complicated than the medical facts. Psychological and spiritual issues are inherent in their situations. Thus, I do not ask these questions about health as a physician would ask them. I ask them as a pastoral caregiver concerned about senior adults' wholistic health. Whether senior adults have become homebound gradually (as a result of progressive scleroderma or arthritis) or abruptly (as a result of a debilitating stroke), they likely continue to experience adjustment issues. As I invite them to talk about those adjustment issues, I use the appropriate parts of the Parish Spiritual Assessment Tool.

Current health conditions and meaning. In the medical component, part II (Health status), I have listed 22 possible health conditions (part II, B) that senior adults sometimes experience in their aging process. Knowledge of these conditions comes from my experience in geriatric ministry. Pastors and other caregivers sometimes fail to recognize these conditions as important because we ourselves do not suffer from them. I provide a list because sometimes pastors and other caregivers, hearing senior adults talk about only one troubling condition, tend to believe that this condition is the member's only health concern. That usually is not the case, however. Many, if not most, homebound senior adults experience multiple health concerns. The list is intended to make it easier (through pastoral conversation) for caregivers to identify how many health problems senior adults have. As the caregiver records the conditions and peruses the notes before a visit, she or he will not only develop a more complete picture of the senior adults' overall health, but will anticipate what needs may occur for them in the future, such as the need for home health care or relocation to an assisted-living facility or nursing home.

It is important to ask senior adults, "What meaning do your health problems have for you?" and "What meaning do they have for you spiritually?" (part II, C, D). Assisting senior adults to find meaning in life and to discover how God's love and presence connect with their past, present, and future is one of the goals of the Parish Spiritual Assessment Tool.

Spiritual meanings of health conditions vary from person to person.

Clarence said, "Every day God gives me is a gift, and I try to make the most of it. I'm 81 years old. Both my parents died in their 60s, so I've outlived them both. I try to live each day as I think God would want me to. God has more for me to do."

"When I was a missionary," Edna said, "I saw a lot of suffering in other countries. I shared God's love with them. I try to do that now also from my apartment. When people come and see me, I tell them how God helps me deal with my suffering. I try to be a missionary to other people right here at home."

Theodore said, "Every night when I go to bed, I wonder if I'll get enough oxygen. My oxygen tank could run out. When my respiratory problems first started, I knew I had to put my house in order. I'm ready to die. I have God's peace."

Power of attorney for health care. While many senior adults reflect on how they will die, some have strong feelings about not wanting to be kept alive by extraordinary medical procedures. Although senior adults often discuss their preferences with the pastor or other caregiver, it is important also to ask people, "Have you granted someone power of attorney for health care? If so, whom?" (part II, E). They may need to be told that unless they have designated someone to speak for them if they become unable to speak for themselves, their medical preferences (as written in their living will) may not be followed. If they have not written a living will, they may want to do so. Discussing this important issue with the caregiver is fine, but their preferences also need to be put in writing, discussed with their family and their appointed agent for health care, and communicated to their physician.

Home health assistance. Raising the question, "What home-health-care assistance do you receive?" (part II, F) may help make senior adults aware of an option that could help them stay in their own homes longer. Sometimes they do not realize such services are available. The caregiver may be able both to provide information about home services and to help seniors find these resources. When caregivers become aware of the number of home services that senior adults receive, they may be better equipped to assess the nature of aging people's neediness as well as to develop follow-up plans for pastoral care.

Observations. I have found it helpful to make my own observations and assessments of how senior adults function physically and cognitively (part II, A, B). My observations do not always coincide with the assessments articulated by the senior adults themselves. This was the case with Harris, who asked, "Can you take this chicken meat off the bone for me? I'm just not having a good day." Because of the possible discrepancy between the caregiver's assessment and senior adults' assessments, I have included in the assessment and plan process in the Parish Spiritual Assessment Tool both part II for the senior adult's agenda and part III for the pastor's or other caregiver's assessment.

Help for the Vulnerable Harris

I knew that Harris probably had become a vulnerable adult. He was no longer able to take care of himself safely. He needed protection from his unavoidable self-neglect. I knew that I needed to take immediate action.

My assessment and plan would need to be done now, in his home. Harris had no family members who lived in the area. He had not spoken with his older son since the young man entered the military as a teenager. The younger son, who called Harris only a few times a year, had moved to Europe as a computer expert for an American company. I knew that I needed to telephone the county adult protection office and report Harris as a possible vulnerable adult.

When adult protection office personnel told me that they would send a case worker to Harris's home in approximately one hour, I told them that I would stay with Harris until the case worker arrived. I called the church office and asked the secretary to let the other senior adults on the day's visitation schedule know that I had an emergency and would reschedule their appointments soon. When the adult protection caseworker arrived and completed her assessment, she said Harris would have to be removed from his home for his own safety. Together we took him to the hospital emergency room for a medical evaluation. He was admitted to the hospital for two days while he was treated for his recent stroke. When he was discharged, he was transferred to an area nursing home. Our next visit took place in the nursing home.

Assessment and Plan Component

I. Professional Objectivity
- A. How do I feel about Harris? I like Harris and feel sad that a stroke and other age-related limitations necessitated nursing home admission. While it is possible to remain a private person in a nursing home, it will be more difficult for Harris to live his preferred private lifestyle there.
- B. Does he have life issues that are similar to mine that would make it difficult for me to be objective? Not at this point. When Harris lived in his own home, I needed to be aware that as a single person myself, I may also become reclusive as I age.
- C. Do I have countertransference issues? No.
- D. Does Harris have transference issues? No.

II. Senior Adult's Agenda
- A. What does Harris want?

1. Spiritually: Harris wants to receive communion and pray in quietness.
2. Psychologically: Harris does not want to interact with other people.
3. Familially: He expressed no wants or needs.
4. Socioeconomically: He does not want social interaction.
5. Medically: He expressed no wants or needs.

III. Pastor's or Other Caregiver's Assessment

A. Spiritual

1. Assessment: Harris wants to receive communion and pray in quietness.
2. Ways to foster growth: Discuss the corporate nature of communion with him. If he chooses not to attend the chapel services, resume bringing him communion in his new location at the nursing home. Advise him that he has the right to close his room door so that he can pray in privacy and in quietness.

B. Psychological

1. Assessment: While Harris prefers no interaction with other people, he may become a happier person if others take an interest in him and he begins to talk with them, even in a limited way.
2. Ways to foster growth: Advise the nursing home chaplain and social worker of Harris's preference. Ask them to consider occasionally paying Harris brief visits, making the visits seem routine. Ask the Agape Visitors from the congregation to do the same as they make their routine, brief visits to our members in area nursing homes.

C. Family

1. Assessment: It might be helpful for both Harris and his sons if they could reconcile with each other.
2. Ways to foster growth: Ask Harris for permission to telephone his sons and update them about the change in his living situation. This contact could help me to ascertain whether reconciliation may be possible.

D. Socioeconomic

1. Assessment: Harris does not want social interaction with other residents.

2. Way to foster growth: Inform Harris that he has the right not to participate in nursing home activities.

E. Medical
1. Assessment: His medical needs are taken care of by the nursing home medical staff.
2. Ways to foster growth: None, unless at some point I perceive a need for Harris to consult a medical specialist and the nursing home does not schedule a visit for him with one. At that point, since he has no family nearby, I may need to be his advocate.

IV. Plan for Responding to the Senior Adult's Needs
A. What church resources are available to address Harris's needs? The pastor (me) and the Agape Visitors.
1. Who is available to contact the Agape Visitors? The office manager.
2. When will the contact be made? Tomorrow.
3. When will the plan be implemented? Next time the Agape Visitors make their nursing home visits.
4. Date on which to provide for follow-up? I will write a note in my appointment book for one month from today to inquire how the lay visitation went with Harris.

B. What community resources are available to address Harris's needs? The nursing home chaplain and the nursing home social worker.
1. Who is available to contact them? Me.
2. When will the contact be made? Today, by telephone.
3. When will the plan be implemented? At their discretion. Also, the next time I visit Harris, I will try to find the chaplain and the social worker and discuss Harris's adjustment to life in the nursing home.
4. Date on which to follow-up? I will schedule myself to visit Harris and these nursing-home staff members one month from tomorrow.

V. Likely Consequences if I Elect to Do Less or More than Expected or Needed
A. Spiritual consequences: None, because Harris will continue to receive communion and will continue to pray.

B. Psychological consequences: If I do not contact the nursing home chaplain, the social worker, and the Agape Visitors, Harris may be less likely to experience happiness. At the same time, however, there will always be nursing home staff who will interact with him as they assist him with his activities of daily life.
C. Family consequences: If I do not obtain permission to telephone Harris's sons, there may be no possibility for reconciliation in the family.
D. Socioeconomic consequences: None.
E. Medical consequences: None, unless a medical specialist is needed.

Nursing home life became the beginning of a very different life for Harris. He "blossomed"! He responded so well to the visits from the chaplain and social worker that he accepted their invitations to expand his contacts and participate in activities in the nursing home. He enjoyed the men's discussion groups and took part in the woodworking class (as well as he could with his physical limitations). As he ate nutritionally balanced meals, he became physically stronger and more cognitively alert. He even began to help another resident assemble jigsaw puzzles.

Physical therapy became one of his favorite activities, because as his muscle tone strengthened, he was able to get around by himself in his wheelchair. As he did so, it was actually difficult to find him when I went to visit because he enjoyed "cruising the hallways." Although he gave me permission to telephone his sons, they expressed no interest in their father. Overall, however, Harris became a happier person in the nursing home because of social interaction, medical care, and improved nutrition. While he was still legally a vulnerable adult, he was not as helpless as he had once been.

CHAPTER 7

Initial Visits in the Nursing Home

While some nursing homes require that formal spiritual assessment forms be included in the charts of new residents, I have found the Nursing Home Spiritual Assessment Tool included in this chapter to be the most effective tool for communicating practical senior adult religious preferences, both to the parish pastor or other caregiver and to the nursing home staff. When the nursing home already has a spiritual assessment form, this Nursing Home Spiritual Assessment Tool can supplement it. The difference between this form and many institutional forms is that this one is intended only to provide practical information. The information obtained from senior adults by the use of this form is communicated primarily to the chaplain or (if there is no chaplain) to the charge nurse.

My goal is to complete this tool during the initial visit with residents. The length of time required for its completion, however, depends on the amount of conversation surrounding each question. Sometimes two visits are necessary. The Nursing Home Spiritual Assessment Tool can be used by parish pastors, lay caregivers, and nursing home chaplains. The goals of caregivers who use the Nursing Home Spiritual Assessment Tool are to:

- Ascertain during the initial visit the types of religious services preferred by residents and their families.
- Collegially communicate (with the resident's permission) residents' religious preferences to the nursing home staff.
- Extend an invitation to higher-functioning residents to participate in a "Blessing of the New Home Service" (chapter 11).

Senior adults' religious preferences are usually communicated either to nursing home chaplains or charge nurses. Chaplains who receive this information will quickly learn which residents want to attend chapel services and Bible studies and which residents have physical limitations that affect their participation, such as visual or hearing impairments or physical weakness.

When nursing homes do not have a chaplain, the parish pastor or lay caregiver shares the senior adult's religious service preferences with the charge nurse. This information will enable her or him to know which residents want to attend public worship and Bible study in the nursing home when pastors volunteer these services, and what assistance the volunteer pastor will need to provide to the residents.

Whenever possible I try to complete the Nursing Home Spiritual Assessment Tool with the help of both the senior adult and his or her family. This practice enables me to learn senior adult religious preferences even when residents have dementia and are unable to speak for themselves. It also gives me the opportunity to offer support to families who have recently made the difficult decision to place a loved one in a nursing home. When families' schedules or other factors preclude concurrent visitation, this assessment may be done with families at another time–perhaps at church, in their home, over the telephone, or (with modifications) by E-mail or fax.

The Nursing Home Spiritual Assessment Tool is used for initial visits only. Follow-up visitation with residents who function well cognitively follows the format of the Parish Spiritual Assessment Tool. If senior adults were previously visited in their homes by caregivers who followed the Parish Spiritual Assessment Tool, that meaningful process will continue during nursing home visits.

Residents who function at a lower cognitive level (because of dementia, injury, or disease), should be offered a ministry of pastoral presence, compassion, love, support, Scripture, and prayer. Such ministry, of course, needs to be offered to all senior adults.

Visiting members in nursing homes should be included in every congregation's senior adult ministry program. The parish pastor and lay visitors remain the primary spiritual care providers for senior adults, even for those who have relocated to nursing homes with a chaplain. The chaplain does not replace the pastor. Senior adults should be visited with the same regularity in nursing homes as they were, or would be, visited in their private homes. They need to be in relationship with their parish and to know that they continue to be important members of their congregation. All senior adults in nursing homes need to be visited by congregational caregivers, whether they function well cognitively, have advanced dementia, are bedridden, or are unresponsive. Nursing home visitation is part of the New Testament mandate that states, "Religion that is pure and undefiled before God, the Father, is this: to care for orphans and widows in their distress" (James 1:27). Many nursing home residents are widows, and some aging people can be considered orphans because they have no families or friends.

Congregations that have a number of members in the same nursing home may wish to hold monthly congregational worship services as a way not only to ensure that members receive Holy Communion regularly, but also to help members maintain a sense of connection with their congregation. Worship leaders may wish to consider the following suggestions for the service.

- Focus on the comforting messages of Jesus' love, rather than on more challenging messages, such as the sinful condition of humanity. It is better for residents at a lower cognitive level (who tend to focus on select words and phrases) to focus on positive words rather than on words that may trouble them.
- Select familiar hymns and prayers that the residents may have learned from memory when they were young. This will increase the likelihood that residents will participate in the service.
- Relate to the residents in a low-key manner and with patience. Project to them both the spoken and unspoken message that you really want to be there and that you are not in a hurry to leave.
- Speak slowly, distinctly, and with enough volume to be heard. If they cannot understand or hear you, they may not attend the next service.
- Remember that some residents may speak at inappropriate times, fall asleep and snore, or develop coughing spells.
- Remember that often the most powerful message residents take with them is how the worship leader responded to their needs during the service. They may need a warm greeting, a kind word, a glass of water, a tissue, a word of clarification, or a dropped book picked up off the floor. Their needs are more important than strict adherence to worship rubrics.
- Give residents additional time to consume the bread and wine. Some residents may have difficulty swallowing and need a small piece of bread or need to have the bread dipped in the wine (intinction). Other residents may prefer grape juice for communion. They may need the officiant to hold the glass for them when they drink.

To encourage pastoral accountability, I keep notes on nursing-home visitation, just as I keep notes on visits with senior adults in other settings. I use the format described in chapter 1 for note-taking, including the assessment and plan process. I keep notes in my laptop computer. I also keep a specific schedule for nursing home visitation on simple graph paper so that I can easily, quickly, and efficiently keep track of my visits. I make regular visits and visit all senior adults with equal frequency, unless an emergency requires extra visits.

Nursing Home Spiritual Assessment Tool

A. Basic Information

1. Name ______________________________ Room__________

2. Date of birth ______________________________

3. Date of admission ______________________________

4. Date of assessment ______________________________

5. What was your primary job in younger years? ____________

6. What is the highest educational level you have completed? ____

7. Whom would you want me to call if you have an emergency?

   ____

8. Where did you live before you came to the nursing home?

   ____

   [The information in a) *through* c) *need be assessed only by the caregiver.]*

   a) ____ Transfer from hospital
      (1) ____ with expectation of progress
      (2) ____ for maintenance
      (3) ____ due to terminal illness

   b) ____ Transfer from another nursing home

   c) ____ Deterioration of health at home

9. Medical information volunteered ______________________

   [for chaplains]:

10. Name of congregation ______________________________

11. Denomination ______________________________

B. Worship

1. Has worship been important to you throughout your life?
2. How often did you attend worship as a child?
3. How often did you attend worship as an adult?
4. How often have you attended worship during the past two years?
5. In what church activities did you previously participate?
6. Would you like to attend chapel services?
   a) *[Provide a printed schedule of chapel services.]*
   b) *[Provide a printed schedule for the congregation's monthly communion service at the nursing home.]*
7. Will your family be able to attend chapel services or our congregation's communion service with you?
8. What are your favorite hymns?
9. Can you see to read large-print hymnals?
10. Are you able to hold a hymnal?
11. Do you have a hearing problem so that sitting near a loudspeaker would be helpful?
12. If you are physically able, would you like to serve in any of the following ways?
    a) Distribute hymnals for chapel services.
    b) Find page numbers for residents who need assistance.
    c) Read Scripture during worship.
    d) Sing in the resident choir.
    e) Collect hymnals after the worship service.
    f) Assist with changing altar paraments.
    g) Provide altar flowers when you have flowers in your room.
    h) Read devotions to visually impaired residents.
13. Would you like to watch or listen to local church services on the television or radio during the week? *[Provide a printed schedule.]*
14. Would you like to listen to religious music in your room?
    a) Do you have a tape recorder [CD player]?
    b) If not, can you obtain a tape recorder [CD player]?
    c) Do you have recorded tapes [CDs]?
    d) *[The congregation may be able to provide a tape recorder and tapes (or CD player and CDs) if the resident or family is unable to do so.]*

C. Sacraments
   1. Have you been baptized?
   2. If have not been baptized, would you like to be baptized?
   3. How often do you like to receive Holy Communion? _________
      [Provide a printed schedule of all available communion services, including chapel services and congregational services.]
   4. Do you prefer wine or grape juice for communion?
   5. If you become unable to attend the nursing home communion services, would you like communion brought to your room?

D. Scripture
   1. Would you like to attend the lay visitor's or chaplain's Bible-study group?
   2. What are some of your favorite Bible passages?
   3. If you are unable to see to read, would you like to have Scripture read to you?
   4. If you are able to see to read, do you read devotions or other spiritual literature?
      [The congregation needs to provide daily devotional books.]

E. Pastor's or Other Caregiver's Observations
   1. Are there religious pictures in the member's room?
   2. Are there religious figurines in the member's room?
   3. Is religious reading material in sight?
   4. Are there religious symbols in the room?

F. Blessing of the New Home Service
   1. Describe the service to residents for whom it is cognitively appropriate.
   2. Ask, "Would you like to have a 'Blessing of the New Home' service?"
   3. Ask, "Do you have family members or friends who may like to attend?"
   4. Ask, "May I telephone these people to extend an invitation to the service?"

G. Pastoral Plan Check List

1. I requested permission from the resident and/or family to share information with the nursing home staff.
2. I informed nursing-home staff of the resident's desire to attend chapel services.
3. I informed nursing home staff about the resident's desire to attend the chaplain's Bible study.
4. I spoke with the nursing home volunteer coordinator and/or church volunteers about the resident's desire to hear Scripture read.
5. I arranged for meeting the resident's request to listen to religious music in his or her room.
6. I called or E-mailed family or friends who may want to attend the "Blessing of the New Home" service.
7. I scheduled a time and date for the "Blessing of the New Home" service that will not conflict with the nursing home schedule.
8. I shared information with the nursing home chaplain.
9. I will do the following for residents who are unable to leave their rooms for worship services or Bible studies:
   a) Visit them regularly and remind them that God loves them.
   b) Read them comforting Bible passages.
   c) Make it possible for them to hear religious music or tapes of the congregation's worship services.
   d) Provide them with lightweight, large-print devotional books.
   e) Pray with them, especially familiar prayers.
   f) Show them comforting pictures of Jesus or other Christian art.
   g) Bring them Holy Communion.

Loving Care for Nursing Home Residents

Even though many books have been written about visitation with nursing home residents and people who have Alzheimer's disease, I have included this chapter about nursing home visitation to emphasize the importance of including members in nursing homes in the pastor's or other caregiver's regular visitation schedule, and to show how nursing ng the Parish Spiritual Assessment Tool. Nursing home residents, like the rest of us, are unique individuals who have been created in the image of God. One day many of us may live in nursing homes. Let us visit nursing home residents with the same kind of love and quality of care that we ourselves will want.

Part III

Responding to Senior Adults' Needs on a Congregational Level

CHAPTER 8

Senior Advisory Committee

It is not unusual for congregations to find that a significant proportion of their members and weekly worshippers are over age 65. According to data released by the United States Administration on Aging, in 1997 the number of people in the United States age 65 or older was 34.1 million, or 12.7 percent of the total population, approximately one in every eight Americans.[1] The agency estimates that by the year 2030 the number will increase to approximately 70 million.[2] People who are 65 and over are projected to represent 13 percent of the population in the year 2000, and 20 percent by 2030.[3] The same office reported that in 1997 the number of people age 85 and older was 3.9 million, 31 times larger than in 1900.[4]

Just as congregational planning is needed in the areas of Christian education, worship, evangelism, stewardship, and social ministry, so too planning is needed in the area of senior adult ministry. Besides providing meaningful home visitation for senior adults by pastors and lay caregivers, congregational planning should include intergenerational worship and programs, education of older adults about the issues of aging, and care of and education for families of seniors. Comprehensive ministry for this age group does not just happen. One effective approach to developing a broad-based congregational senior adult ministry is to form a senior advisory committee.

Selecting Committee Members

The majority of the senior advisory committee must be senior adults because people in this age group are most familiar with the issues of aging. While the pastors and the younger lay leaders of the congregation have ideas about the needs of senior adults and may presume to know what they need and want, only members who experience the issues of aging themselves can address these issues outside the purely cognitive realm and connect them with the practical struggles of daily life. During meetings of the senior advisory committee, the senior adult committee members raise issues of concern for the aging, assist in developing and implementing a ministry to address them, become vocal advocates for the needs of the older members of the congregation, and develop new forms of ministry to meet the needs of seniors. The senior advisory committee neither fosters dependence on the congregation nor independence from the congregation. Instead, it fosters a healthy interdependence.

Senior adult members from a variety of backgrounds should be recruited to serve. It is helpful if committee members can represent at least some of the following life situations: a homebound member, a member who becomes homebound during extreme weather (hot summers or cold winters), a widow, a widower, an active married couple, a caretaker spouse of a homebound spouse, an adult son or daughter who takes care of a homebound parent, an employed senior adult, a recent retiree, a spouse or adult child of a nursing home resident, a member who lives in a senior high-rise or other retirement facility, a member with legal expertise, a wealthy member, a low-income member, and a middle-income member who does not qualify for public assistance of any kind. Members from these life situations should be encouraged to contribute to committee discussions both from their specific life situations as well as from their personal perspectives.

Other senior advisory committee members may also be recruited. It is strategic to have a member of the congregation's worship committee serve on the senior advisory committee and to act as a liaison for senior adult worship preferences. It is also strategic to have representatives from the congregation's women's and men's organizations who can serve as liaisons with these often large groups.

Developing a Job Description

After the senior advisory committee members are recruited, logistical details such as day and time of meetings can be established. Other matters, of course, are determined by the committee job description, which can be written before members are recruited. A sample job description for the senior advisory committee is as follows:

Preamble: All persons have worth and dignity because they are created out of God's love and in God's image. [Name] Church unconditionally values our senior adult members. We recognize that while they are united in their belief in the crucified and risen Jesus Christ, they are diverse in talents, experience, interests, and needs.

Responsibilities: To highlight the importance of our congregation's senior adult ministry, the senior advisory committee will strive to:

1. Ensure and enable the spiritual nurture of our senior adult members.
2. Strengthen the bond between our senior adult members and other members of our congregation.
3. Encourage, enable, and empower our senior adult members to share their faith, wisdom, experience, and talents with our congregation.
4. Advise the visitation pastor about senior adults whose changing life situations now require home visitation by the pastor and lay visitors.
5. Educate our entire congregation regarding the nature and value of our senior adult members and the issues of aging.
6. Enlist our congregational members to reach out to our senior adult members.
7. Keep our congregation informed about the effect of congregational worship, events, and programs on the lives of senior adults.
8. Keep our congregation informed about the effect of current events, social issues, and social policies on the lives of senior adults, as well as encourage that these concerns be addressed through sermons, adult forums, newsletters, and other formats.
9. Educate the families of our senior adult members about the issues of aging and offer support to families.
10. Help plan and carry out innovative fellowship activities for our senior adult members.

The senior advisory committee will be a primary committee of the congregation and will have voice and vote representation on the congregational council.

The preamble describes the congregation's valuation of its senior adult ministry. It indicates that while there are similarities among senior adult members, diversity is also characteristic of this important segment of the congregation. As such, it recognizes that congregational programs need to address the uniqueness of individual senior adult members, as well as their common needs and wishes. As the congregation is educated about the diversity of needs and wishes among senior adults, stereotypical ideas about aging people may be banished. The responsibilities of the senior advisory committee need to address accurately the needs and wishes of the congregation's senior adults. The responsibilities may be periodically modified.

Developing a Meeting Agenda

The senior advisory committee agenda might include the following items:

1. Devotions related to senior adult ministry
2. Roll call of committee members
3. Secretary's report
4. Treasurer's report
5. Brief report from the committee on new referrals of senior adults who may need pastoral visitation or assistance from the congregation. (Situations can change on a daily basis for senior adults, and the pastor alone cannot keep up with the changing needs.)
6. Brief report on feedback from the congregation about senior adult wishes or concerns (for example, reducing the amount of standing during worship or adding social opportunities).
7. Old business
8. New business
9. Confirm date of next meeting
10. Closing prayer

Just as the responsibilities of the senior advisory committee need to be personalized for each congregation, so does the committee meeting agenda.

Addressing Spiritual Needs

The senior advisory committee oversees many areas of the congregation's spiritual nurture of its senior adults. For example, it ensures that the regular visitation of senior adults by pastors and lay caregivers is meaningful by recommending that the visitation follow the format (as described in this book) of the Parish Spiritual Assessment Tool and the Nursing Home Spiritual Assessment Tool. This recommendation emphasizes the importance of high-quality visitation in which senior adults are assisted to find meaning in life, to apply proven inner resources to current and future life needs, and to experience the love and peace of God. The senior advisory committee provides training sessions and refresher sessions for lay visitors based on this format for visitation.

Sunday morning worship needs of senior adults who are able to attend worship are addressed by the senior advisory committee. Many of these are detailed in chapter 2. Additional worship needs which the committee will address include:

- Making the worship experience more physically comfortable through the use of pew cushions.
- Inviting senior adults to serve as ushers, communion assistants, and lectors.
- Reducing the amount of standing during worship.
- Including familiar hymns in the worship service.
- Including senior adult concerns in sermons and prayer petitions.
- Offering communion stations at the bottom of the steps leading to the altar so that those who would like to come forward for communion but are unable to climb steps are accommodated.
- Bringing communion to disabled members in the pews.
- Celebrating communion with grape juice (instead of wine) for those who are diabetic or on medications that preclude alcoholic beverages.

The senior advisory committee will address Sunday morning worship needs for homebound adults in the following ways:

- Encouraging the congregation to broadcast the congregation's worship service on the radio and cable television.
- Recruiting a church volunteer to deliver a quantity of Sunday bulletins to each retirement setting in which senior adult members reside.
- Encouraging members who live in retirement settings to sit together to watch or hear the broadcast, using the bulletins previously delivered.
- At the conclusion of the congregation's Sunday morning communion service, sending out trained and authorized lay communion assistants to bring communion to homebound members, using the consecrated elements from the service.

The senior advisory committee will ensure that all hospitalized and homebound senior members, whatever their living situation, receive communion. The committee will watch for opportunities for pastors and trained and authorized lay ministers to celebrate communion with groups of members who live in retirement settings. The officiant may choose to schedule several services in one afternoon. It is best to schedule these services on the same day each month so that the pastor or lay minister will keep the time block available and so that the members can look forward to that time.

It is important that the senior advisory committee members or other members appointed by the committee (youth can participate during the summer months) join the officiant for the monthly group communion services as a way of reminding the homebound members that the entire congregation, not just the pastor, cares about them. When the congregation has a large number of senior adults in retirement settings, the pastor should also attempt to schedule one-on-one visits with these members on a regular quarterly or semiannual basis, unless senior adults encounter crisis situations requiring more immediate pastoral visitation. Lay visitors might visit more frequently. When Holy Communion is brought to private homes, the pastor or lay minister should occasionally bring another member along (with the senior adult's permission, of course) as a way of emphasizing to the homebound member the communal nature of the sacrament.

The senior advisory committee member who is also on the congregation's worship committee may recommend to that committee that the spiritual needs of senior adults be further addressed by scheduling a number of daytime worship services throughout the year. Noontime Lenten services will enable those senior adults who cannot drive after dark, those who are concerned about their safety after dark, those who need to take public transportation, and those who have more energy in the afternoon than in the evening, to attend midweek worship. Another advantage of scheduling Lenten services over the noon hour is that younger members may be able to attend on their lunch break.

Additional quarterly or semiannual afternoon worship services with Holy Communion which are held in the church will be scheduled throughout the year for homebound members. For these services, the senior advisory committee will enlist assistance from other congregational committees to organize transportation and refreshments. The fellowship time following the worship services is important for senior adults who are most often isolated at home and have little one-on-one contact with other friends and members from their church.

Other needs to be addressed by the senior advisory committee might include the following:

- Invite senior adults to join a prayer chain coordinated by telephone, a prayer group that meets in homes, or a communal prayer group that meets at the church.
- Establish a dedicated telephone line for a Dial-a-Prayer recorded message with the opportunity to leave personal prayer requests.
- Form faith-sharing groups for senior adults, using the Spiritual Journey Exercise for Small Groups (included on accompanying CD-ROM).
- Provide rides for senior adults so that they can participate in meetings of the congregational women's and men's groups.
- Make large-print Bibles and cassette recordings of the Bible available through the church library or through individual purchase.
- Include senior adults on church committees.
- Schedule church meetings during the daytime when possible.
- Provide an adequate number of parking spaces reserved for the handicapped and disabled.
- Prepare large-print church newsletters.
- Place padded chairs in meeting rooms.
- Supply safety devices for the handicapped in restrooms.
- Install an elevator.
- Host an annual outing for senior adults.
- Advocate for senior adults through the governmental political and legislative process.
- Give special attention to senior adults who are unable to articulate their needs and concerns.

Addressing Psychological Needs

While neither the senior advisory committee nor the congregation can respond adequately to all the psychological needs of senior adults, some steps can be taken. The committee can seek to address loneliness and depression in senior adults in the following ways.

- A Be-a-Friend Program will be organized to match lay caregivers who are trained in one-on-one visitation with senior adults who are lonely and depressed. The volunteers visit monthly and otherwise stay in touch with senior adults on a regular basis (for example, by telephoning, running errands, or sending cards). The Be-a-Friend Program may include a traveling Bible study, which the pastor writes each month for the caregiver to use during visitation.

- An Agape Visitors Program will use church volunteers who prefer a less structured visiting schedule than the Be-a-Friend Program. The volunteers can informally visit senior adult members in homes and in retirement facilities, at the convenience of the volunteers and with no promises for follow-up visits at specific intervals. This program supplements the Be-a-Friend Program and seeks primarily to address loneliness in senior adults.
- Various congregational organizations will be encouraged to provide occasional programs for senior adult members who live in retirement facilities. Refreshments and conversation will follow the program. These events will address senior adults' issues of loneliness and isolation.

Other psychological needs will also be addressed by the senior advisory committee as new programs and events are organized.

- A Telecare Program will be organized to reduce the anxiety of senior adults who live alone. Church volunteers telephone senior adults daily at the same time to ensure that they are all right.
- The congregation will serve holiday communal meals for those who live alone and may experience holiday loneliness, as well as provide rides to the meal.
- A Christmas Service of Comfort and Remembrance (see chapter 10) will be held to address holiday grief. Rides will be provided to the service.
- Congregational support groups will be organized for widows and widowers, caregivers of senior adults, those who are working through grief, family and friends of loved ones with Alzheimer's, and sons and daughters who are primary caretakers for one or both parents.
- An adopt-a-grandparent program will be coordinated with the Sunday school and confirmation classes. This program, which addresses senior adults' needs for intergenerational relationships, also educates youth about the value and wisdom of aging people.
- A computer station with Internet connections will be established in the church library for senior adults to use for E-mailing relatives and for exploring their connection to the global world.

Addressing Medical, Physical, and Social Needs

The senior advisory committee will encourage the congregation to address medical, physical, and social needs of senior adults in the following ways.

- Members of a TLC (Tender Loving Care) group will be available to perform a variety of good deeds for senior adults. Such services may include helping senior adults make telephone calls to businesses or companies when they have difficulty speaking, thinking, or hearing over the telephone; reading correspondence or the newspaper to visually impaired senior adults; and writing letters for those whose arthritis or visual impairment makes that difficult.
- Free blood-pressure readings will be offered on Sunday mornings; at the Lunch Bunch (a group of senior adults who eat lunch together once a month, each time at a different handicapped-accessible and reasonably priced restaurant); at meetings of Senior Lites (a group of senior adults who meet once a month in the evening for a potluck meal, devotions, structured meeting, and program); and at meetings of Elderberries (a group of senior adults who meet monthly for games, crafts, video movies, therapeutic hand massages, programs, and refreshments).
- A parish-nurse program will be implemented.
- Catalogs of special need items will be available from the church office (such as clothing with Velcro closures, large-digit telephones, large-print books, extra-loud alarm clocks and telephones, large-handled eating utensils, kitchen convenience items, and bathroom safety items).

Addressing Family Members' Needs

The senior advisory committee will invite family members to join senior adults for various worship opportunities as family schedules permit. Family members who participate will not only worship and receive Holy Communion together but also will learn more about the spirit of their older relative and experience an even closer bonding. Families who live near their senior adult can be encouraged through a mailing from the senior advisory committee to attend monthly home communion with their family member during Sunday morning worship, communion services in retirement facilities, or home communion. For family members who live far from the church and may be unable to attend the monthly communion services, the well-publicized annual congregational “Bless the Years” Sunday (see chapter 9) will offer this opportunity. Printed invitations will be sent to families far in advance so that travel plans can be made.

The senior advisory committee will also address support and education for families of the congregation’s senior adult members. These ideas will need assistance from congregational leaders.

- The congregation may commit itself to develop or house a community adult day care program, a meals-on-wheels program, or a congregate dining program.
- A respite-care program may be developed. Church volunteers offer caregivers of homebound senior adults the opportunity to leave the house for a day, a half-day, or even a couple of hours. This time away will be used by the caregiver for self-care. The respite-care program will include monthly or quarterly meetings for mutual support, education about strategies for self-care, and fellowship for home caregivers.
- The senior advisory committee will coordinate adult education programs on issues of aging, such as Alzheimer’s, death and dying, funeral planning, help in the Bible for particular life situations, depression, hospice, tips for visiting in a nursing home, suggestions for adapting a home environment to physical limitations, nutrition, pre-retirement, and retirement.

Community Resources and Programs

The senior advisory committee and pastors need to be aware of existing community resources and programs for seniors. The congregation may or may not wish to duplicate some of these programs. Two organizations from which the senior advisory committee and pastors can receive assistance in caring for senior adult members are the Interfaith Caregivers Program and the Area Agency on Aging.

The Interfaith Caregivers Program is a national program of caregiving supported by the Robert Wood Johnson Foundation. Local interfaith coalitions help people with disabilities to stay in their homes by providing home-based care and support through a network of trained volunteers. As part of this program the local coordinator works with religious organizations, including congregations, to ensure that senior adults receive support for such needs of daily life as companionship, transportation, shopping, personal care, chores, and referrals to other relevant community services.

Area Agencies on Aging were mandated through a 1973 revision of the federal Older Americans Act. The legislation requires every locality to have an Area Agency on Aging. The agency serves as an advocate for the elderly within the federal government, as well as it works to develop a system of family and community-based services throughout the nation. The local agency can serve as an information and referral source for congregations and assess the needs of senior adults.

A Comprehensive Ministry

Congregations that want to provide an effective senior adult ministry will not only include home visitation but will also develop other congregational programs and events. Because comprehensive senior adult ministry does not just happen, the congregation will organize a senior advisory committee to ensure that extensive ministry to aging people does take place.

The senior advisory committee plans, coordinates, and implements wholistic ministry for the congregation's senior adults and its intergenerational membership. It strives to incorporate into all group and congregational events the same one-on-one goals used in the congregation's home visitation using the Parish Spiritual Assessment Tool. This approach will ensure that the congregation has a coordinated senior adult ministry program that values and affirms the dignity and diversity of the congregation's senior adults. As the world's senior adult population grows, it is imperative that congregations develop senior advisory committees.

CHAPTER 9

Bless the Years Sunday

I have come to believe that every congregation that has senior adults in its membership needs to hold an annual "Bless the Years" Sunday. This special Sunday represents on a congregational level ministry goals similar to those that the pastor and lay caregivers have for one-on-one visits with senior adults in home visitation through the use of the Parish Spiritual Assessment Tool.. The Bless the Years Sunday is intended:

- To bless senior adults.
- To affirm the worth and dignity of senior adults.
- To help senior adults experience meaning on a congregational level by proclaiming the intergenerational message that every year added to a person's life is a gift to be celebrated.
- To help younger members relate to their elders with sensitivity and care in the spirit of Jesus Christ.

These purposes are addressed through a thematic Sunday morning worship service that includes a special printed order of worship, a children's sermon focusing on the meaning of blessing, a sermon for adult worshippers focusing on the theme of the day, a blessing spoken by younger members to older members, and a return pledge from the older members to the younger. Samples of all these items are included in this chapter.

This chapter includes suggestions for how to plan a Bless the Years Sunday. Other ideas are available from the Association of Lutheran Older Adults. ALOA is the only nationwide Lutheran ministry devoted exclusively to affirming and challenging people as they grow older. The organization points out: "[I]n a culture that is quick to dismiss or disregard people as they grow older, the church remains the single rallying point where young and old, the strong and the fragile, the impaired and the agile, are to be welcomed, included, inspired, and engaged for faithful response to the invitation of Christ Who calls, 'Come!' and His awesome assignment, 'Go!'"[1] Many of the ideas in this chapter, including the bulletin resources and part of the children's sermon, are from ALOA and are used with the association's permission. The sample adult sermon is written by the author.

Planning

Set a date. After a congregation has designated a specific date for the "Bless the Years" Sunday, whether it be in May during Older Americans Month, in September on Grandparents Day, on the Sunday following Rally Sunday, or another Sunday, sufficient planning time needs to be allowed. The timeline in this chapter, of course, can be modified.

Three to six months in advance. I have found that having the senior advisory committee (chapter 8) coordinate the planning is helpful. Since this committee plans and coordinates the congregation's senior adult ministry, it can closely connect the congregational goals for senior adult ministry with the purposes of the Bless the Years Sunday. This ongoing committee can also ensure that the Bless the Years Sunday becomes an annual event, that the planning and coordination will have continuity, and that these will be efficiently carried out from year to year.

During the early planning phase, the committee will decide whether it wants to focus exclusively on the worship service or whether it wants to provide additional programming. When the senior advisory committee decides to add programming for the day, some suggestions may include:

- Inviting an outside speaker who is an expert in the area of geriatrics or geriatric ministry to present a program for an adult forum.
- Creating an intergenerational event that can build deeper bonds among the generations in the congregation.
- Holding a senior adult resource fair to raise awareness about community resources. While this can take months of planning and coordination, the time is well spent because the event can help senior adults and their families obtain needed psychological, medical, home health, financial, and legal services. Our congregation had representatives from 25 organizations that serve senior adults present for our senior adult resource fair.

- Holding a congregational potluck meal and inviting the senior adults to be guests of honor. Great care needs to be taken so that all senior adults are invited, greeted when they arrive, and shown to their places of honor for the meal. A short program may be included. During the program, the oldest senior adults in the congregation may be recognized. Senior adults who feel comfortable speaking in public may share a few words about what their faith means to them.

The main tasks at this early stage of planning are to set a date and to decide what the Bless the Years Sunday will include so that the event can be put on the church calendar and so that resource people can be invited and the event added to their schedules.

Two months in advance. Designate an age to be used to define the term "senior adult" for the Bless the Years Sunday. Committee members may have differing opinions. The designated age will be used to develop a list of senior adults who are to be invited to the worship service through written and telephone invitations. This age will be determined by the demographics of the congregation. If the membership overall is old, the designated age may be 65, 75, or even older. I have found that 65 is a safe choice because it is a typical age at which senior adults begin to receive Social Security checks.

When committee members develop the list of senior adults, they should plan to keep the master list for future use. Then rather than generating a new list, the committee will need only to modify it, adding names, changing addresses and telephone numbers, and deleting the names of those who have died or left the community.

Six weeks in advance. Begin to write the order of worship, make specific plans for any additional programming that has been scheduled, decide who will provide refreshments for the coffee hour and contact that person or organization, find a transportation coordinator and volunteer drivers, find a telephone coordinator and telephone volunteers, make publicity posters for the church and other public places, write publicity articles for the church newsletter, and prepare an advance publicity article for the local newspaper, radio, and cable television stations.

The nature of the worship service needs to be given prayerful thought. If the congregation does not serve Holy Communion on a weekly basis, it is important to hold the Bless the Years Sunday on a communion Sunday so that senior adults who are usually unable to get to church will be able to receive the sacrament on this special day when transportation is provided. Inviting senior adults to serve as worship leaders may be meaningful in congregations that have aging members who are comfortable and articulate in public speaking. In other congregations, such speakers may be unavailable, or senior adults may prefer just to listen on the day when they are honored. In some congregations senior adults may feel comfortable serving as greeters, ushers, lectors, and communion assistants; in others they may not wish to serve in these roles. Of course, in congregations that have a primarily older membership, senior adults may serve in these capacities every Sunday. In some congregations, a special choir of singers over the designated age may be formed for the day, while in older congregations members of the regular church choir may already be over the designated age. Hymns for the day may be selected from the current hymnal or from a retired hymnal.

Approximately one month before the Bless the Years Sunday, give the order of worship and other bulletin information to the church secretary. This will enable the secretary to manage the office schedule and allow time for the senior advisory committee and pastor to proofread the bulletin and make last minute changes.

Four weeks in advance. Prepare the invitations to be mailed to the designated senior adults. By the time senior adults receive this invitation, they will probably have read about the Bless the Years Sunday in the church newsletter, heard it described during radio and cable television broadcasts of the worship services, and read about it in the local newspaper. A sample form for the invitation:

> *Dear Senior Adult Friends in Christ,*
>
> *You are important to us! We love you, and Jesus loves you!*
>
> *Please join us at Our Savior's Lutheran Church on Sunday, September 21, for our Bless the Years Sunday! This is a day when our entire congregation honors and blesses you.*
>
> *Our Bless the Years worship service will include a hymn sing 15 minutes before each service, a special order of worship, special music, a sermon that focuses on the theme of the day, and Holy Communion.*
>
> *Between the worship services* [here additional events are described]. *Refreshments will be served in the Fireside Room.*
>
> *Invite your family to join you for this blessed day.*

You will be contacted by telephone so that transportation can be provided for you if you need a ride.

God bless you and God bless this special day!

Prepare a telephone script to invite senior adults to worship on the Bless the Years Sunday. The script may be similar to this:

My name is ______________________. *I am a member of* ______________________*Church and am a member of the* [senior advisory committee]. *As you know from the invitation you received in the mail, we are having a special day on Sunday, September 21, to bless and honor you and the other senior adults in our congregation. We are calling this event the Bless the Years Sunday. It is a day when we give thanks to God for the added years of life which God gives to our senior adults and to all of us. We know that it is not always possible for you to attend church on Sunday mornings, but we really hope that you can attend on September 21. To make it easier for you to attend, I am calling to offer you a ride to either the 8:30* A.M. *or 11:00* A.M. *worship service. I will make the arrangements for you, if you need a ride. Do you need a ride? Which service would you like to attend? Please be ready for the volunteer driver 30 minutes before the service. I am glad that you will attend. God bless you.*

Include publicity in church newsletters and weekly bulletins. The newsletters and bulletins may include invitations that senior adults can give to their children, as well as invitations their children can give to them. The latter invitation can also be used by any member of the congregation to extend an invitation to a senior adult friend or neighbor.

The printed invitation that senior adults may wish to give to their children may state:

Dear [Daughter/Son],

You know that my faith has always been a very important part of my life, just as your faith is important to you. You also know that Our Savior's Lutheran Church is very important to me, just as you are important to me. I would like to invite you to join me for worship at Our Savior's on Sunday, September 21. On this Sunday we are celebrating our Bless the Years Sunday. It is a day when our church honors and blesses its senior adult members. That includes me now. Each worship service (8:30 A.M. and 11:00 A.M.) will focus on this theme. Holy Communion will be served. It would be wonderful to worship and commune with you. I hope that we can attend together. If we are able to arrive 15 minutes early, we can take part in the "old favorites" hymn sing. I love you!

The printed invitation which children (or grandchildren) may wish to give to parents (or grandparents) may state:

Dear Mom/Dad,

Not only are you important to me, but you are important to our congregation, Our Savior's Lutheran Church. I would like you to be my honored guest at the Bless the Years Sunday on Sunday, September 21. This will be an opportunity for us to worship and receive Holy Communion together on a day when senior adults are specially blessed and honored. This will take place at both the 8:30 A.M. and 11:00 A.M. services. I will pick you up early for whichever service you prefer so that we can enjoy the "old favorites" hymn sing before the worship service begins. I love you!"

If your worship service is not broadcast on radio or television, make arrangements to videotape or audiotape the Bless the Years Sunday, as well as to mass-produce the tape. Recruit volunteers to deliver a copy of the tape, a church bulletin, and refreshments from the coffee hour to homebound senior adults.

One to two weeks in advance. Mail the invitations to senior adults. If aging members who have any degree of dementia receive the invitations earlier than this, it is likely that either the invitations will be lost or the senior adults will become confused about the date of the service. Also, divide the mailing list among the telephone volunteers. Provide the written script for the telephone volunteers, and instruct them when to make the calls and when to report to the telephone coordinator their results about who needs a ride.

The telephone coordinator will make sure that all the names on all the lists have been called. Telephone calls should be made approximately four days before the Bless the Years Sunday. If senior adults are telephoned earlier, they may be unable to give a definitive answer because they will not be able to predict how they will be feeling on the designated Sunday. Even when the calls are made four days in advance, senior adults may legitimately say the same thing. The telephone coordinator reports the results to the transportation coordinator, who matches the names of senior adults who need rides with volunteer drivers.

One week in advance. Advise the head usher that extra ushers will be needed on the Bless the Years Sunday because some senior adults have physical impairments and will need assistance. Ushers will be needed at the church doors to meet and greet the senior adults, as well as to lend a supportive arm or offer the use of a wheelchair. Ushers also will be needed in the sanctuary to lend support to senior adults who want to walk to the altar for communion, especially if there are steps in the chancel.

Additional worship service accommodations will be needed. A supply of large-print bulletins should be available for those with visual impairments. A communion station may be placed at the base of the altar steps to preclude the necessity of walking up the steps. An announcement can be made that the pastors will bring communion to the pews for senior adults who inform an usher of the need.

Order of Worship

The following order of worship may be considered for a "Bless the Years" Sunday. The litany, prayer of the church, and "Bless the Years" text were written by the Association of Lutheran Older Adults.

HYMN SING: The singing can begin 15 minutes before the worship service and include such favorite hymns as "Softly and Tenderly Jesus Is Calling," "What a Friend We Have in Jesus," "Blessed Assurance," and "Sweet Hour of Prayer."

ANNOUNCEMENTS: The senior adults are recognized, and the theme of the day is explained.

PROCESSIONAL HYMN: This hymn can be another favorite, selected by the senior advisory committee.

Pastoral Greeting

Pastor: The grace of the Lord Jesus Christ, the love of God, and the communion of the Holy Spirit be with you all.
People: And also with you.

Litany

Pastor: O God, whose children we are, help us recall all the ways and times you have proved to be our loving parent.
People: For it is you, God, who provided us with those who cared for us in infancy, affording shelter, protection, nourishment, and care, while we neither realized these were our needs nor knew who they were who gave us such care.
Pastor: O God, whose children we are, help us recall the joys of our childhood.
People: For it is you, God, who have surprised us with the color of sunsets, the brightness of stars, the fragrance of flowers, the songs of the birds, the laughter of friends, the warmth of the beds that welcomed us after exhausting play, and the soft voices of those who spoke with us our evening prayers.
Pastor: O God, whose children we are, help us recall your protecting hand attending us as years have passed.
People: For it is you, God, who brought healing to our scratches and our bruises and our pains, recovery from illnesses, renewed spirit after disappointments, and warded off dangers and disease that threatened our well-being.
Pastor: O God, whose children we are, help us recall the times you have stood close by when sorrows crowded in on us.
People: For it is you, God, who gave your Son for us, experiencing deep pain and loss; who know and feel our every loss, assuring us that you will never leave us nor forsake us in our heavyheartedness.
Pastor: O God, whose children we are, help us to see the gift that is ours in the family of the church.
People: For it is you, God, who looked beyond what we have been, who in the waters of baptism marked us as your very own, members of your family, and sisters and brothers of one another.
All: O God, whose children we are, help as we grow older, to grow wiser, to grow in our thankfulness, and to grow in our sense of responsibility, so that we may use the gifts of grace, experience, skill, time,

and all our resources for service to you and our neighbor, through Jesus Christ, our Savior. Amen.

FIRST SCRIPTURE READING : Num. 6:22-27

CHILDREN'S SERMON. (A sample sermon is included in this chapter.)

SPECIAL MUSIC

SECOND SCRIPTURE READING: Eph. 1:3-4

HOLY GOSPEL READING: John 13:31-35

SERMON: The sermon follows the theme for the day. The preacher strives to deliver a message for all ages. (A sample sermon is included at the end of this chapter.)

HYMN

PRAYER OF THE CHURCH

Pastor: Let us pray for the whole people of God in Christ Jesus and for all people according to their needs.

People: We praise you, O God, for the mystery of your presence among us. Remind us always of your presence in the lives of all your people. Especially this day we remember you in the lives of the senior adults among us. May we honor them and you with love.

Pastor: Let us pray for all who give care directly and personally in our homes and all settings of ministry.

People: Grant, O God, tenderness and tenacity, insight and imagination, patience and perseverance to all who give intimate care. May it be done as unto you.

Pastor: Let us pray for all who receive care.

People: Kind and loving God, it is not easy to have the tables turned–to receive rather than to give care, to need a reassuring touch rather than to share one, to be weak when we would like to be strong. Give us graciousness to receive care in your name.

Pastor: Let us pray for the families of our senior adults.

People: O God, on the cross you remembered your mother to the beloved disciple, saying to him, "Here is your mother." Mature and strengthen us so that we in like mind may lovingly see to the needs of

those who have cared for us.
Pastor: Let us pray for ourselves as we age.
People: We pray that you will keep us in touch with our own aging. Help us to value our years both as a gift and as a chance to give.
Pastor: O God of Compassion, we pray for all those in special need this day, especially do we name before you. . . . God, in your mercy.
People: Hear our prayer.
Pastor: Into your hands, O God, we commend all for whom we pray, trusting in your mercy; through your Son, Jesus Christ our Lord.
People: Amen.

Bless the Years

Pastor: Now a word to all who have not yet reached the age of 65 *[or whatever age the committee has designated]*. Since you have recognized the gifts God has given you on your journey through the years–your friends, the people dearest to you, moments of special and warm remembering, God's entrance into your life in Holy Baptism, the awesome but exhilarating tasting of bread and sipping of the cup at Supper, the constant and repeated assurances that God will never leave or abandon you, I therefore ask all of you, do you this day now pledge anew to celebrate God's love to you in Christ Jesus, with praise and thanksgiving, remembering especially those older and their needs, welcoming their wisdom, cherishing their friendship, remembering them to be temples in whom God has chosen to reside, seeking ways to include them in our planning and working together to serve God and our neighbor! Please respond loudly.
People: With the help of my empowering God, I so pledge.
Pastor: And now a word to all whom God has given added years beyond the age of 65 *[or designated age]*. Since you have recognized the gifts God has given you on your journey through the years–your friends, the people dearest to you, moments of special and warm remembering, God's entrance into your life in Holy Baptism, the awesome but exhilarating tasting of bread and sipping of the cup at Supper, the constant and repeated assurances that God will never leave or abandon you, do you this day in baptismal confidence now pledge, individually and with others, to celebrate God's love to you in Christ Jesus, with praise and thanksgiving, and to seek new expressions of service that promote healing, reconciliation, growth, and justice?

People: I so pledge, asking God to support me in this in the name of Jesus Christ my Lord.
Pastor: Thanks be to God.
Congregation: Amen.

OFFERTORY

SACRAMENT OF HOLY COMMUNION

BENEDICTION

RECESSIONAL HYMN

Sample Children's Sermon

Who can tell me what this is? *[Birthday cake.]* This is a picture of a birthday cake, isn't it? How many of you have had real birthday cake? If I were to put these two candles on the birthday cake, what would they mean? *[Someone is two years old.]* If I were to put four candles on the birthday cake, what would they mean? *[Someone is four years old.]* If I were to put six candles on the birthday cake, what would they mean? *[Someone is six years old.]*

Some of our church members who are here this morning are over 65 years old. If we had a cake for someone 65 years old, how many candles would we need? *[Sixty-five.]*

Many people in our church have celebrated a lot of birthdays. Some have had more than 70 or 80 or 90 birthdays. That's a lot of birthdays.

We have a church member who lives in a nursing home named Sally. Sally is 102 years old. How many candles would Sally need on her cake? *[102]*.

Our members who are over the age of 65 are being blessed today in church. They were little children like you at one point in their lives, and they learned about Jesus in Sunday school and church just as you do. But they did not stop learning about Jesus during their lives. For all their years, they continued to read their Bibles, attend worship, and pray to Jesus. Jesus is with us throughout our entire lifetimes.

Do you know how to sing? Do you know how to sing "Happy Birthday"? It goes like this, doesn't it? *[Sing it.]* Now, I would like to teach you another verse of the "Happy Birthday" song. It goes like this: "God's blessings to you. God's blessings to you. God's blessings, dear friends. God's blessings to you." When we sing it like this, we are praying that God will bless the person for her or his whole life.

Now, I would like you to sing it with me to our older members, OK? And, let's have all our members who are under the age of 65 sing it with us. Here we go: "God's blessings. . . "

Remember that God will be with you all your life. You may go back to your pews now. Thanks for coming up.

Sample Adult Sermon

First Scripture Reading: Num. 6:22-27.
Second Scripture Reading: Eph. 1:3-4.
Holy Gospel Reading: John 13:31-35.

Grace to you and peace from our crucified and risen Jesus Christ. Amen.

A special welcome is extended this morning to all senior adult members at Our Savior's Lutheran Church. This is a special day for you, and this is a special day for our congregation. Today we honor you, our senior adults; and today we bless you. You are important to us! We value you! We cherish you! We give thanks for you!

Who are our senior adults? At what age is one considered a senior adult? The senior advisory committee, which met with me to help plan this special day for you, carefully selected the age of 65, because that is the usual age at which a person first receives monthly Social Security checks. Yet there are other ways of defining the age of a senior adult, are there not?

If we look at the candidates in the 1996 presidential election, we find that when President Bill Clinton turned 50, he became a card-carrying member of the American Association of Retired Persons. He might then have been considered a senior adult. At age 72, Bob Dole, Clinton's presidential challenger, ran an energetic and vital campaign. Thus, we see that there is no single age at which one is considered a senior adult.

Senior adults are "seasoned" adults. Throughout their lifetimes they have turned time and time again to the promises of God for guidance, comfort, and strength in life. Senior adults are seasoned Christian "recyclers." They continue to recycle the promises of God so that those younger than they are can learn from them to count on God in Christ. Senior adults are seasoned "role models of faith" from whom others can learn Christian wisdom.

Yes, today we bless you, our senior adults. What does it mean to bless someone? Sometimes when we conclude a visit with a friend, we may say, "God bless you," as we leave. Sometimes if someone sneezes, we may say, "God bless you." Sometimes at Christmas we may wish one another not only a merry Christmas, but also a blessed Christmas.

To bless someone–that is to say, today, to bless our senior adults–is biblical. In the Old Testament, God blessed people with God's presence and promise; that presence powerfully delivered them from times of hardship, danger, and trouble. In our first lesson for today, God commanded Moses to be the vehicle of God's blessing, as he said to the people: "The Lord bless you and keep you. The Lord make his face to shine upon you, and be gracious to you. The Lord lift up his countenance upon you and give you peace."

In the New Testament we see that the concept of blessing was modified to mean specifically God blessing people through Jesus, as we heard in our second lesson for today. "Blessed be the God and Father of Our Lord Jesus Christ, who has blessed us in Christ with every spiritual blessing."

Yes, in the New Testament Jesus becomes the One who blesses. Jesus blesses the little children. Jesus blesses his disciples as he sends them out on mission and tells them to greet others with a blessing. Jesus blesses people through his miracles and as he reduces people's anxiety. Jesus blesses the five loaves of bread and two fish when he feeds more than 5,000 people. Jesus blesses the bread and wine at his Last Supper with his disciples before he is crucified. Jesus blesses his disciples before he ascends into heaven.

Today, we the disciples of Jesus at Our Savior's Lutheran Church bless our senior adult members. In fact, following the prayer of the church this morning, I am going to ask all worshippers under age 65 to stand and respond to a pledge printed in the bulletin. This pledge recognizes the gifts God has given our senior adults and the gifts they have shared with us. In this process, those of us under age 65 pledge to you, our senior adults, that we celebrate God's love for you, welcome your wisdom, and cherish your friendship. As we so bless you today, please know that we respect and love you. We also impart power to you. We say to you today that we not only care about you, but we need you. We are grateful for all the years of Christian worship and service which you have given to your church and to your God; and we are grateful for your ongoing worship and service.

After we have made our pledges to you, we will ask you to make two pledges. First of all, we will ask you to pledge to celebrate the love which God has given to you through Jesus Christ. Secondly, we will ask you to continue to share your Christian gifts and wisdom with us.

Sometimes after turning 65 and retiring, a person may question his or her role in life, especially if limitations develop. We at Our Savior's Lutheran Church say to you today that whether or not you have developed limitations, you are important to us! We value you for who you are! We value you for your God-given being.

It is like the story told of the woman who visited the great sculptor Michelangelo. She watched as he used a hammer and chisel on a lovely, large block of marble. She was grieved to see him chipping away at the large stone. She objected and pointed to the growing pile of marble chips that littered the floor. However, Michelangelo said, "The more the marble chips fall, the more the beautiful statute inside grows."

While limitations may develop and chip away at that which you would like to be able to do, your inner spiritual being becomes more and more beautiful as you mature in faith and become more like the spiritual image of God. This is part of the beauty of faith.

Yes, on this Bless the Years Sunday, while we at Our Savior's Lutheran Church bless you, we can be likened to Moses in our first lesson, because today we are vehicles of God in Christ for you. As we bless you, know that it is Jesus himself who blesses you.

Jesus blesses you with his omnipresence here in this holy sanctuary and in your homes. Jesus blesses you with companionship, protection, strength, and compassion. Jesus blesses you with his divine love, which is with you now and will be with you in eternity.

As Jesus so blesses you with companionship, love, strength, hope, and peace, remember that you continue to become more and more like the spiritual image of God. Thus, today I say this to you, our senior adults. You are loved and cherished and blessed by your congregation, Our Savior's Lutheran Church; and you are loved and cherished and blessed by your Lord and Savior, Jesus Christ. Amen.

CHAPTER 10

Christmas Service of Comfort and Remembrance

The Christmas Service of Comfort and Remembrance, a ministry of the senior advisory committee, provides an intergenerational worship opportunity for those who have experienced the death of a family member or friend in the past year. People in other ministry settings–groups of congregations, assisted living facilities, and nursing homes–will also find this annual service to be a creative form of pastoral care. The service can be adapted and offered as a quarterly memorial service in each setting. It can also be adapted for use on All Saints' Sunday, the day when the church has traditionally remembered those who have died in the past year.

The purposes of the Christmas Service of Comfort and Remembrance are:

- To comfort senior adults and people of all ages who have experienced the death of a loved one in the past year.
- To provide practical suggestions for surviving the first Christmas without the deceased loved one.
- To comfort those who have experienced deaths in past years to continue to deal with their holiday grief.
- To offer an opportunity during the fellowship hour for those who grieve to share their feelings with others who also grieve.

When the Christmas Service of Comfort and Remembrance is held in a church, the senior advisory committee takes the leadership role in planning, coordinating, and leading the event, as well as in educating the congregation about the purposes of the service. The worship service includes a litany of remembrance, a sermon with practical ideas for dealing with holiday grief, presentation of ornaments placed on the church Christmas tree that carry the names of those who have died, prayers of comfort, and appropriate Advent hymns and Christmas carols. Samples of all these items are included in this chapter. The committee may request assistance from other congregational committees for the events of the day. For example, the fellowship committee can coordinate the refreshments, and the property committee can obtain the Christmas tree.

Planning

Six months in advance. Schedule the Christmas Service of Comfort and Remembrance at least six months in advance, and make sure the event is on the church calendar. The Advent-Christmas season is busy! Coordinate the date of the service with the pastor's preaching schedule. Hold the service as soon as possible after Thanksgiving, so that grievers will be able to draw comfort and strength from it for as long a time as possible during the holiday season. Schedule the service for a Saturday or Sunday afternoon so that employed people and family members who live at a distance are better able to attend. Also schedule the organist, the soloist (instrumental or vocal), and the committee that will provide refreshments following the service.

Four months in advance. Order the worship bulletins and Christmas tree ornaments from a church-supply catalog. Select medium-size, unbreakable Christmas tree ornaments, preferably flat to make them easier to mail to families unable to attend the service. Allow for a space on which to write the name of the deceased. Wooden ornaments are often easy to write on and do not break in the mail. If plastic ornaments are used, it may be necessary to write the name on a small label and affix it to the ornament. Determine how many ornaments will be needed to place on the tree and to present to the families during the service. While one ornament per family will be placed on the Christmas tree, order additional ornaments, because more deaths will occur after the order is placed. Often when there is more than one surviving family member, several people wish to have a keepsake ornament. Find someone who can write the names on the ornaments in an elegant calligraphy a week before the service.

Two months in advance. Prepare the invitations for families who experienced a death in the past year. A sample form:

Dear _______,

God's peace be with you. We at the church know that this will be the first Christmas for you since the death of your loved one. We would like to invite you and your family members to a special worship service called the Christmas Service of Comfort and Remembrance. This will be a time for you and others in our congregation who have also experienced the death of a loved one in the past year to hear God's message of comfort and hope, to remember your loved one, and to share your grief with others who also grieve. The service is open to anyone who would like help dealing with holiday grief.

The Christmas Service of Comfort and Remembrance will be held on Saturday afternoon, [date], at 2:00 P.M. in our church sanctuary. When you arrive for the service, you will see an ornament with your loved one's name on the Christmas tree. During the worship service this ornament will be presented to you. A fellowship hour with refreshments will follow the worship service. You will have an opportunity to talk with others whose Christmas also is different this year.

Other family members or friends who were close to your loved one are also welcome to attend our service. Please invite them! We have mailed only one invitation to each family.

We pray that you will be comforted during the holiday season by knowing that your congregation shares your grief and offers you our support. May you also be comforted with the message of the Babe of Bethlehem, who was born into our world to share our humanity (including our grief) and to give us the divine comfort of God's love.

God bless you,

Your church family

Prepare articles for the church newsletter and Sunday bulletins. These articles may state the following:

[Name of church] *will hold its annual Christmas Service of Comfort and Remembrance on Saturday,* [date], *at 2:00 P.M. in the church sanctuary. All who have experienced the death of a loved one in the past year, as well as all who need help with holiday grief, are invited to attend.*

Letters will be mailed to families of members who died in the past year, indicating that an ornament will be placed on the Christmas tree with their loved one's name on it. The ornaments will be presented to the families during the worship service. If others would also like an ornament placed on the tree in memory of your loved one, please telephone the church office before [date] *so that arrangements can be made. Also telephone the church office if you need a ride to the service. A fellowship hour will follow the worship service.*

Six weeks in advance. Mail the invitations to the immediate surviving family member of each member who died. Assign one committee member to mail additional invitations to families who experience a death after the first invitations have been mailed. This committee member will make sure that ornaments are prepared for those members. Begin to advertise the Service of Comfort and Remembrance in the church newsletter and the Sunday bulletin. Assign another committee member the task of finding volunteer drivers, should they be needed. This committee member will periodically call the church office to inquire if anyone has requested a ride.

Four weeks in advance. Once again speak with the pastor, organist, soloist, and refreshment committee to remind them of the event. Begin to write the order of worship for the bulletin. When designing the service, keep in mind that the length of the service will be determined primarily by the length of the sermon and by the time needed for presentation of the ornaments. Give the order of worship to the church secretary several weeks before the service so that the senior advisory committee will have time to proofread the bulletin and make final changes.

Two weeks in advance. Ask the head usher to secure enough ushers so that one or two can be located at the church doors to assist handicapped worshippers.

One week in advance. Make an alphabetical list of those of have died. This list will be used during the worship service during the presentation of ornaments. Continue to update the list to include the most recent deaths. Designate members of the senior advisory committee to assist with the distribution of ornaments during the service. As the worship leader reads the name of the deceased, one committee member will find the ornaments on the tree and two other committee members will bring the ornaments to the families in the pew where the families stand when they hear their loved one's name read aloud. If the committee chooses to make additional ornaments available to other family members, make plans for how that will be accomplished. Designate a committee member to mail the ornaments to families who did not attend the service.

The day of the service. Before the worship service, place the ornaments in alphabetical order on the Christmas tree so that they can be located quickly.

Order of Worship

The following order of worship may be followed.

PRELUDE

WELCOME

CALL TO WORSHIP

Blessed be the God and Father of our Lord Jesus Christ who is the source of all mercy and consolation. He comforts and strengthens us in all our sorrows so that we can comfort and strengthen others with the consolation we ourselves have received from God.[1] Amen.

PRAYER

Receive our thanks, O God, for the blessed earthly relationship which we shared with our loved ones who are not with us for Christmas this year. Grant that our memories of the life we shared together will remain clear and beautiful. As we continue to grieve, give us courage and strength to face this holiday season. We give thanks that through your humanity you understand and empathize with all our feelings and needs; and, through your divinity you comfort us with the promise of eternal life for all who believe in Jesus Christ, the Babe of Bethlehem. Amen.

OPENING HYMN: "Oh, Come, Oh, Come, Emmanuel"

Oh, come, oh, come, Emmanuel, And ransom captive Israel,
That mourns in lonely exile here Until the Son of God appear.
Rejoice! Rejoice! Emmanuel Shall come to you, O Israel.

Oh, come, blest Dayspring, come and cheer
Our spirits by your advent here;

Disperse the gloomy clouds of night,
And death's dark shadows put to flight.
Rejoice! Rejoice! Emmanuel Shall come to you, O Israel.

Oh, come, O Key of David, come, And open wide our heav'nly home;
Make safe the way that leads on high, And close the path to misery.
Rejoice! Rejoice! Emmanuel Shall come to you, O Israel.

LITANY OF REMEMBRANCE:[2]

Pastor: At the rising of the sun and its going down we remember our loved ones.

People: At the blowing of the wind and in the chill of winter, we remember them.

Pastor: At the opening of the buds and in the rebirth of spring, we remember them.

People: At the blueness of the skies and in the warmth of summer, we remember them.

Pastor: In the rustling of the leaves and in the beauty of autumn, we remember them.

People: At the beginning of the year and when it ends, we remember them.

Pastor: When we are weary and in need of strength, we remember them.

People: When we are lost and sick at heart, we remember them.

Pastor: When we have joy we crave to share, we remember them.

People: When we have decisions that are difficult to make, we remember them.

Pastor: When we have achieved goals based upon the values that they taught us, we remember them.

People: As long as we live, they too will live; for they are now a part of us, as we remember them.

SCRIPTURE LESSONS: Eccles. 3:1-8, 1 John 4:13-16, Matt. 11:28-30

SERMON: (A sample sermon is included at the end of this chapter.)

HYMN: "Angels We Have Heard on High"

Angels we have heard on high,
Sweetly singing o'er the plains,

And the mountains in reply,
Echoing their joyous strains.
Gloria in excelsis Deo;
Gloria in excelsis Deo.

Come to Bethlehem and see
Him whose birth the angels sing;
Come, adore on bended knee
Christ the Lord, the newborn King.
Gloria in excelsis Deo;
Gloria in excelsis Deo.

PRESENTATION OF ORNAMENTS[3]

Pastor: We remember today our family members and friends who have died.

People: Although they are not physically with us, we rejoice in the memory of their love.

People: O God, we thank you for our family members and friends whom we have been remembering–for all that made them unique and for the gifts they have passed on to us and to the world through us. We give thanks for the gift of peace, which they now enjoy in the eternal kingdom. Amen.

Member of Senior Advisory Committee: As I read your loved one's name and take an ornament bearing the name off our church tree, please stand so that it can be brought to you. You can put it on your tree or place it in a special location in your home.

CLOSING PRAYER

Pastor: We give thanks for the life we had with our family members and friends who died this past year. We give thanks for their special traits, values, faith, affection, love, joy, laughter, and companionship. Help us as we grieve to make their gifts and love part of our lives as a living memorial. Bless us with the light of promise, courage, comfort, rest, strength, and hope of the Babe of Bethlehem. As we give you thanks for the gift of the promise of eternal life, help us to sing along with the angels at that first Christmas, "Glory to God in the highest, and on earth peace to all people." Amen.

LORD'S PRAYER

Benediction

The Lord bless you and keep you. The Lord make his face shine on you and be gracious to you. The Lord look upon you with favor and give you peace. Amen.

Closing Hymn: "Oh, Come, All Ye Faithful"

Oh come, all ye faithful, Joyful and triumphant!
Oh, come ye, oh, come ye to Bethlehem;
Come and behold him Born the king of angels:
Oh, come, let us adore him, Oh, come, let us adore him,
Oh, come, let us adore him, Christ the Lord!

Sing, choirs of angels, Sing in exultation,
Sing, all ye citizens of heaven above!
Glory to God In the highest:
Oh, come, let us adore him, Oh, come, let us adore him,
Oh, come, let us adore him, Christ the Lord!

Postlude

Sample Sermon

First Lesson: Eccles. 3:1-8
Second Lesson: I John 4:13-16.
Holy Gospel Reading: Matt. 11:28-30.

Welcome to our Christmas Service of Comfort and Remembrance. I am pleased that you are here. It may not have been easy for you to attend our service today. While you made the decision to come and receive comfort, you may also have dreaded coming because you did not want to stir up the painful grief you have been experiencing. These days and weeks before the first Christmas without your dear loved one can be difficult. Things are different this year. You are bereaved. You miss your loved one. Your pain is great because you know that you will never again enjoy family traditions or new experiences with your loved one.

We who are here this afternoon know the primary One to whom we turn for understanding, comfort, consolation, hope, and peace. We turn to the One who has invited us to come unto him for rest. Yes, in this holy season of the church year, Jesus, the Babe of Bethlehem, gives us the gifts of his divine comfort, rest, and peace.

We who are here this afternoon also give one another the gifts of compassion and support. We understand one another. And as Christian people, we know that our Lord Jesus Christ, the Babe of Bethlehem, brings divine comfort, strength, and hope to our shared understanding and compassion for one another.

In this season of gift-giving I would like to talk about three gifts this afternoon. The first gift is the gift of time. Our Old Testament reading for today reminds us that time is divine. The author of Ecclesiastes writes that there is a time to be born and a time to die . . . there is a time to weep . . . there is a time to mourn . . . there is a time to build up [and a time to heal] . . . there is a time to embrace . . . and a time to love . . . there is a time for peace. My friends in Christ, time is a gift.

I encourage you to give yourself the gift of time. Give yourself the gift of time to grieve. There is no use trying to pretend that Christmas this year is like any other Christmas. It is not like other Christmases because of the death you have experienced.

The author Washington Irving said, "There is a sacredness in tears." During this holiday season, while there may be times when you can tell you will shed tears, there may be other times that tears will come when you least expect them. Tears need to flow freely. One father understood that his children would continue to miss a dear friend, even months and months after the friend's death. The father said, "When we are talking about him [the friend] at the table, sometimes my kids start to cry. I'm so glad they can do that. Then we do it together." Allowing yourself to share tears with another person can be helpful because through the sharing, some of the loneliness will lessen.

Yes, I encourage you to give yourself the gift of time to grieve. It may be that as you try to make Christmas preparations, as you write out a gift list, as you shop, as you hear a favorite carol, as you plan your Christmas Eve and Christmas Day dinners, as you put up a tree or choose not to put up a tree, as you miss buying your loved one a present, as you decide to modify how you observe Christmas this year, or as you do something even unrelated to Christmas, your emotions may feel as though they are "snowing you in" all at once. You may feel numb, sad, empty, confused, overwhelmed, angry, or fearful. These are normal responses to the loss of a loved one.

As you give yourself time to grieve, you may consider doing one or more of the following to get yourself through the holiday. As you consider these suggestions, select the ones that work for you. Remember that no two people grieve in exactly the same ways. Here are some suggestions to consider.

- Look at a photo album and remember positive experiences you had with your loved one.
- If you have a family videotape, view it.
- Line up cherished gifts that your loved one gave you.
- Play music that reminds you of her or him.
- Write down your feelings.
- Place a wreath on the grave.
- Bring a favorite picture of your loved one to your Christmas gathering and explain why this picture is important for you and what memories it brings to mind. Talking together is very important.
- Use a special bowl or piece of silverware from your loved one for your Christmas dinner.
- Cook your loved one's favorite food as a way of cherishing the memory. If this stirs too many emotions, you may wish to select a different menu this year.
- Say your loved one's name aloud a number of times.
- Give yourself permission to say no. Accept invitations and tasks only as you have the energy. Listen to your heart. You will not always feel the way you do this year Do not force yourself to do something you do not want to do.
- On the other hand, do not deny yourself the enjoyment of activities and companionship if you so desire. Your loved one would want you to have a fulfilling and blessed Christmas.
- Consider shopping by catalog instead of fighting the traffic and store crowds. This may relieve you of one burden this year.
- Consider doing something special in memory of your loved one. This might include giving church flowers or a church radio broadcast for Christmas, or it might include a donation to charity.
- Recognize how far you have come. Give thanks for the special strengths you have found within yourself and which you have been given. Congratulate yourself for getting out of bed on the days that seemed impossible. Give yourself credit for learning to manage the everyday stuff of

life without your loved one, who once was an integral part of your daily life.

- Eat well-balanced meals. If you do not feel like cooking, go out to eat.
- Exercise as you are able, because exercise burns up stress.
- Remember that the use of too much alcohol will be detrimental.
- At the same time, because grief takes a lot of energy, rest when you need to do so.
- You may find it helpful to lower your expectations of yourself and build flexibility into this year's Christmas to give yourself time to grieve adequately.

Yes, the first gift I invite you to consider today is that of giving yourself the gift of the time to grieve; and as you take time to grieve, be kind and gentle with yourself. Treat yourself as you would care for your best friend in a time of need.

The second gift which I invite you to consider today is the gift of who your loved one was to you. You knew your loved one well.

Ask yourself the following questions, and perhaps talk about them with people around you. What were your loved one's special traits? What were his or her virtues? What were his or her values? What did you learn about life from her or him? What did you learn about faith from her or him? Think of the intangible gifts which your loved one gave you, such as affection, love, joy, laughter, and companionship.

Keeping in mind that although no one is perfect, the world needs everything you can share with it of the good and unique things about your loved one. That is the gift of self which your loved one shared with you. As you incorporate your loved one's values and passions into your own life and as you pass them on to others, you create a living memorial that will keep alive the essence of your loved one and will bring you comfort.

The third gift I invite you to consider today is God's gift to you–God's gift of the Babe of Bethlehem, Emmanuel, "God with us." The Babe of Bethlehem was born into a symbolically dark world. Just as God entered the darkness of the world, God tells you that God does not abandon you in your darkness. And God does not abandon you in your times of need. As we read in our second lesson for today, "God abides in those who confess that Jesus is the Son of God, and they abide in God."

Friends in Christ, God blesses you by dwelling within you in the deepest and most personal level of your being. Once you have seen God in a stable, you can never be sure where God will appear, and you can never be sure to what lengths God will go to find you and minister to you. It may be that God comes most fully where you least expect God: in your grief, bringing you promise; in your fear, bringing you courage; in your loneliness, bringing you comfort; in your suffering, bringing you strength and hope. Yes, the Babe of Bethlehem, who was born in the darkness of night, brings the light of promise, courage, comfort, strength, and hope to you.

Remember the following during these difficult days, yet these very holy and blessed days.

- Remember that it is God's intention for you to make it through these difficult days.
- Remember that you are not required to apologize for your feelings or for your tears.
- Remember that God is able to bring you healing. Healing takes time, but God is doing that. That is partly why you are here today. Healing is not about forgetting. Healing is about remembering.
- Remember that there is no end to God's power or your privilege to draw upon it for you healing.
- Remember that you are not lacking in faith because you are feeling sorrowful.
- Remember to pray. Ask your pastor, family, and friends to pray for you. If formulating words is difficult, pray the Lord's Prayer or other written prayers.
- Remember to depend upon God, because that is what God in Jesus Christ is here for. As Jesus says, "Come unto me and I will give you rest."
- Remember that the God who became flesh is also the God who gives the gift and promise of eternal life.

And remember that just as the angels of heaven sang at that first Christmas, so too they sing to you today, "Glory to God in the highest, and on earth, peace to all people"–to all people–and that means you! Amen.

CHAPTER 11

Blessing of the New Home Service

The Blessing of the New Home Service is a ministry of the senior advisory committee that helps senior adults who move into new homes to realize that neither God nor their family or congregation will abandon them. Although I use this service primarily in nursing homes, it also can be used in assisted-living facilities and other apartment buildings. As this ritual connects senior adults' emotions with God's love and blessings, senior adults feel more at peace and develop a greater acceptance about living in their new home.

The Blessing of the New Home Service relates directly to the Nursing Home Spiritual Assessment Tool described in chapter 7. At the conclusion of the initial visit, using the format of the Nursing Home Spiritual Assessment Tool, an invitation is extended to senior adults who function at a high cognitive level to have the pastor or other caregiver conduct the Blessing of the New Home Service in their room on another day.

Sometimes the caregiver learns during the initial visit (using the Nursing Home Spiritual Assessment Tool) that residents were admitted to the nursing home only for convalescent care. These senior adults, of course, do not consider the nursing home to be their new residence. If they later decide they are unable to return home, the pastor or other caregiver will offer to conduct the service for them. In other situations, when senior adults are distressed about needing to live in a nursing home, the pastor or lay caregiver needs to delay the invitation until a higher level of acceptance has been reached. These delays can take one or two months, or even longer. Parts of the service need to be modified slightly when a delay occurs.

Caregivers may experience special challenges with residents who function at a limited cognitive level. For example, residents with dementia may indicate a desire to participate in the service, yet on the day of the service, they may forget both that the service is to be held and what the service is about.

An explanation of the service, as well as a renewed invitation to participate in it, needs to be given again. For these senior adults, the poignant "moment" of the blessing service is more important than their ability to remember later that they participated in it. This service is inappropriate for senior adults with advanced Alzheimer's disease. The Blessing of the New Home Service may also be inappropriate for newly admitted residents who are terminally ill.

Planning the Service

Scheduling the date and time. Consult with the facility staff before setting a date and time for the service so that when the worship leader arrives, the senior adult will be available. When senior adults live in a nursing home and their families want to participate in the service, the service can be scheduled to follow a resident care conference to minimize the amount of time family members need to take off work.

Chairs. During the initial visit, count the number of chairs in the room where the Blessing of the New Home Service will be held. It may be necessary on the day of the service to locate additional chairs and bring them to the room.

Candle. In whatever type of facility the service is held, using a battery-operated candle is practically advantageous, so that the pastor or other worship leader does not need to remember to bring matches or deal with warm candle wax after the service. If the service is held in a nursing home room and the caregiver prefers to use a real candle, inquire if it is legal in your state to do so.

Music. When making the cassette tape of music for the service, have a male vocalist sing the recommended hymns. Male voices are more discernable than female voices by hearing-impaired people. While it may initially seem that making a tape of the church choir singing the hymns would be most enjoyable for senior adults, the words are less likely to be clearly audible. It is important that senior adults hear the words of the recommended hymns, because their message coordinates closely with the theme of the service.

Participation of others. When a facility staff person, another tenant or resident, family member, member of the senior advisory committee, or facility chaplain participates in the Blessing of the New Home Service, provide a copy of the recommended words they will speak, so that they will have time to see whether they agree with the statement and so that they will be prepared for their turn to speak.

Presentation of gift. Congregations may want to purchase an inexpensive cross that can be presented to the senior adult at the conclusion of the service. The cross will be a memento of the service and will remind the resident of God's love and the congregation's love. Select a four- to six-inch cross that can either be hung on the wall or placed on a nightstand or dresser.

Personalizing the Service

As the pastor, lay caregiver, or chaplain leads the Blessing of the New Home Service, she or he needs to personalize the service beyond the printed words. Take the liberty to ad-lib and to engage senior adults in brief conversation during the service to help to make the service especially meaningful for senior adults and their families.

Blessing of the New Home Service Liturgy

Name of Senior Adult ______________________________

Name of Facility ______________________________

Name of Worship Leader ______________________________

Date of Service ______________________________

Worship Leader:

We begin in the name of the Father, Son, and Holy Spirit [*make the sign of the cross*]. Amen. We have gathered today to bless [*name(s) of senior adult(s)*]'s [new] home at [*name of facility*]. This may be a time of mixed feelings for you. You may have feelings of grief and loss over your changing health needs [which made it necessary to leave your previous home]. You may feel anxious about what life will be like in your new home, as you meet caregivers and other residents and as you adjust to a new schedule. On the other hand, you may feel relief in knowing that now you do not need to clean, grocery-shop, cook, and do laundry. You also may feel more secure in knowing that someone is near you 24 hours a day. You are not alone. God is with you during this time of change.

[*The worship leader lights a candle.*]

As I light this candle, I ask you to remember your baptism. Just as you were created in God's image and were claimed by God in baptism, God's promise to love you and be with you forever means that God in Christ will give you strength as you adjust to your new home.

SCRIPTURE: Isa. 43:1-5 (paraphrased)

But now thus says the Lord who created you and formed you, Do not fear, for I have redeemed you. I have called you by name, [*name(s) of senior adult(s)*]. You are mine. When you pass through the waters, I will be with you; and through the rivers, they shall not overwhelm you. For I am the Lord your God, Your Savior. You are precious in my sight, and honored, and I love you. Do not fear, for I am with you.

PRAYER:

Our gracious God, we pray that you will bless [*name(s) of senior adult(s)*] and [her/his/their] new home with your divine presence. Help [her/him/them] turn to you and those around [her/him/them] in trust and hope. Though [her/his/their] circumstances have changed, give [her/him/them] strength to accept this change. Help [her/him/them] to find continued meaning and goodness in life so that [she/he/they] will always find fulfillment in you; through Jesus Christ we pray. Amen.

Staff member:

My name is ______________________________. I work as a ______________. On behalf of the staff, I welcome you to our [*name of facility*] family. You are a unique creation of God who has special needs and wishes. We as a staff will care for you well! We invite you to let us know how you feel and what you need. We hope that the adjustment for you [and your family] will be an easy one. As you join our home, may you be blessed. [*The staff person shakes hands with the resident.*]

Tenant or resident of the facility:

My name is ______________________. On behalf of the tenants [residents] at [*name of facility*], I welcome you as a new friend, and look forward to having you join us for conversation, meals, and activities. May you be blessed through the friendships you make here and the new opportunities that you will enjoy here. *[The resident shakes hands with the new resident.]*

Family member [optional]:

(I [We] know this is a difficult adjustment for you. It also is a difficult adjustment for me [us]. It is not easy.) I [We] will continue to be here for you, just as I [we] was [were] with you in the past. I [We] love you. We will continue to be blessed as a family whose members love and support one another. [*The family member gives the new resident a hug or gently squeezes her or his hand.*]

Facility chaplain:

On behalf of the community of faith at [*name of facility*], I welcome you. While you and the other residents continue your church membership in your home congregation, I invite you also to worship here with us and attend our Bible studies. May you be blessed and continue to grow in faith here in our home. [*The chaplain shakes hands with the new resident.*]

Pastor, lay caregiver, or member of the senior advisory committee:

You are an important and valued member of our congregation. We look forward to visiting you here in your new home. Because we know that it is difficult for you to attend worship in our church, we hope that you will feel free to worship here. While you worship here, you continue to be a member of our congregation. We will continue to visit you, bring you Holy Communion, and support you in faith. May you be blessed as you grow spiritually in your new home. [*The pastor or lay caregiver shakes hands with the member.*]

RECORDED HYMN: "O God, Our Help in Ages Past"

Worship Leader:

Just as was true of your previous home, [*name(s) of senior adult(s)*], here at [*name of facility*] many areas of your new home are significant.

[*The worship leader walks to the door.*]

At this door to your room we read from Psalm 121:8, "The Lord shall keep your going out and your coming in, from this time on and forevermore." Let us pray. O God, protect and guide [*name(s) of senior adult(s)*] as [she/he/they] enter[s] and leave[s] [her/his/their] room. Make all [her/his/their] comings and goings enjoyable experiences. Keep [her/him/them] safe day and night; through Jesus Christ our Lord. Amen. I make the sign of the cross upon your door as a sign of God's divine blessing.

[*The worship leader walks to the sitting area.*]

In this sitting area of your room we read from John 13:34, "I give you a new commandment, that you love one another. Just as I have loved you, you also should love one another." Let us pray. O God, bless all visits that [*name(s) of senior adult(s)*] has [have] with loved ones in [her/his/their] room [and by telephone]. Make the visits uplifting and encouraging, so that they renew and refresh [*name(s) of senior adult(s)*] in mind and spirit; through Jesus Christ our Lord. Amen. I make the sign of the cross upon this sitting area as a sign of God's divine blessing.

[*The worship leader walks to the window.*]

In this area of light at the window of this room we read from John 8:12, "Jesus spoke to them saying, 'I am the light of the world. Whoever follows me will never walk in darkness but will have the light of life.'" Let us pray. O God, we give thanks for the light which comes into [*name(s) of senior adult(s)*]'s home through this window. May this light remind [her/him/them] of the goodness of your creation, and of the light of hope and peace which you give [her/him/them] each day. Fill [her/him/them] with the light of life; through Jesus Christ our Lord. Amen. I make the sign of the cross upon this window as a sign of God's divine blessing. Amen.

[*The worship leader walks to the sleep area.*]

In this sleep area of your home we read from Psalm 4:8, "I will both lie down and sleep in peace; for you alone, O Lord, make me lie down in safety." Let us pray. O God, bless this sleep area so that it may be for [*name(s) of senior adult(s)*] a place to fall asleep easily in your tender love and care, a place to sleep all through the night, and a place to arise rested and renewed for a new day with you; through Jesus Christ our Lord. Amen. I make the sign of the cross upon this sleep area as a sign of God's divine blessing.

[*The worship leader walks to locations of the senior adult's personal possessions.*]

[*Name(s) of senior adult(s)*], you carefully chose personal items to bring with you to your new home. These treasured items are more than objects because your cherished memories are attached to them. We read from Luke 12:34, "For where your treasure is, there your heart will be also." Let us pray. O God, your gifts to us are many. Bless the cherished keepsakes which [*name(s) of senior adult(s)*]brought with [her/him/them] to [her/his/their] new home. May the memories associated with them be a constant source of strength, comfort, and blessing; through Jesus Christ our Lord. Amen. I make the sign of the cross upon your treasured keepsakes as a sign of God's divine blessing.

Holy Communion *may be served. Some senior adults and families may not have received communion together recently.*

The Lord's Prayer

Our Father, who art in heaven, hallowed be thy name, thy kingdom come, thy will be done, on earth as it is in heaven. Give us this day our daily bread; and forgive us our trespasses, as we forgive those who trespass against us; and lead us not into temptation, but deliver us from evil. For thine is the kingdom, and the power, and the glory, forever and ever. Amen.

Recorded Hymn: "Bless This House"[1]

Benediction:

The Lord bless you and keep you. The Lord make his face shine upon you and be gracious to you. The Lord look upon you with favor and give you peace. I make the sign of the cross upon [*name(s) of senior adult(s)*] as a sign of God's divine blessing and love, in the name of the Father, Son, and Holy Spirit. Amen.

Explanation of the Service

Liturgical sign. The "Blessing of the New Home Service" begins with the invocation and the sign of the cross. This liturgical sign is used throughout the service to help senior adults remember that the presence of God's love is with them in all areas of their new home. The worship leader always makes the sign of the cross slowly, in reverence and in faith.

Naming. The senior adults are named many times throughout the service. Naming the new residents not only personalizes the service for them, but also indicates that they are important.

God's presence. The opening paragraph describes possible feelings that senior adults may experience in their new home. Great effort, however, has been made not to ascribe feelings to residents. Descriptions about their possible feelings of grief and loss, as well as possible feelings of relief and security, are indicated by the word "may." The primary goal of the Blessing of the New Home Service is to focus on the assurance of God's love and care in the new home. The statement "God is with you during this time of change" is made emphatically, because God's faithfulness can be trusted. God's ongoing presence is also affirmed by the reference to baptism (for those who are baptized), in the Scripture readings, and in the prayers.

Facility staff participation. The worship leader may not be able to include a facility staff member in this service. Staff people may not be allowed to participate because of the time the service takes away from their regular duties. It may be necessary for the worship leader to speak with the manager or administrator of the facility to obtain permission for staff participation.

Tenant/resident participation. When the congregation has more than one member who lives in the facility, the worship leader may wish to ask another member to take the tenant or resident role in the service. I have found that residents enjoy participating in this service because they get to meet a new resident, to invite him or her to activities, and to assure new residents that there are new opportunities in life.

Family participation. Before the service, the worship leader should discuss with families whether they wish to make a statement to their loved one during the service and whether the recommended printed statement is congruent with their intentions for visiting their loved one. The worship leader may encourage families to improvise their statements, if they wish. Senior adults and their families often become tearful during this part of the service.

Chaplain's participation. The statements by the worship leader and chaplain, especially the phrases "community of faith at [name of facility]" and "your church membership in your home congregation," are important. The participation of both the congregation's pastor and the facility chaplain affirms to senior adults that while chapel attendance is encouraged, their church membership remains in their home congregation.

Hymns. The recommended hymns assure senior adults of God's presence in the new living environment. The hymn "O God, Our Help in Ages Past" assures senior adults that the omnipresent God who has been with them in the past continues to be with them in the present and will be with them in the future. The closing hymn, "Bless This House," is a musical summary of the Blessing of the New Home Service.

Specific blessings. Whether senior adults walk with the worship leader to the door, the sitting area, window, and bed depends on their physical condition and the size of the room. Each respective location is blessed as the Bible verse and prayer are offered, and the sign of the cross is made.

The pastor or other caregiver will want to find out before the service whether senior adults brought personal items with them. Omit this part of the service in a nursing home setting if you observe no personal items.

Holy Communion. Holy Communion may be welcomed by senior adults and their families. If the family is from a different congregation or a different community, families may not have had the opportunity to commune together for a long time. When senior adults were previously homebound, their families may not have been present when the communion minister brought the sacrament. Holy Communion is meaningful during the Blessing of the New Home Service because it draws senior adults and their families closer to God and to one another during their adjustment to life in a new home.

Climax of service. The service concludes with the familiar Lord's Prayer, the hymn "Bless this House," and the benediction. The benediction proclaims the final blessing of the service. The climax of the service occurs when the worship leader makes the sign of the cross upon senior adults as they are named and blessed in the benediction. A cross may be presented to senior adults at the conclusion of the service.

Marking a Poignant Time

It is a tender moment both for senior adults and their families when aged people move into a nursing home or apartment after many years of living in the same home. Hopes and fears abound. I have found that this Blessing of the New Home Service not only helps the adjustment, but also encourages senior adults and family members to share their feelings about this change that affects them all.

APPENDIX A

Spiritual Journey Exercise for Individuals

When congregations prepare this exercise for members, they may wish to allow more space between questions for individuals to write their responses.

Note: The primary purpose of the Spiritual Journey Exercise is to help individuals to reflect on their faith journey. In the process senior adults will develop an understanding of how God has been with them in the past, is with them in the present, and will continue to be with them in the future, providing strength, meaning, and peace. Senior adults may wish to write their answers. For those who desire, the answers can be typed into a spiritual autobiography, spoken into a tape recorder, or videotaped. Then the completed exercise can be presented to family members as a gift.

I. Church Background

A. How long have you been a member of your current congregation?

B. If you have been a member of other congregations, which congregations were they?

1. Did you notice differences in beliefs and religious practices in these congregations?
2. What differences did you notice?

C. What do you appreciate most about being a member of your current congregation?

II. Worship

A. How often did you attend worship during (1) childhood and youth, (2) young adult years, (3) mature adult years, and (4) the past two years?

1. Weekly
2. Two to three times a month
3. Once a month
4. Several times a year
5. On holidays
6. Never

B. If you did not attend regularly what was your reason?
1. Transportation limitations
2. Weather
3. Structural factors at the church (for example, too many steps, heavy doors, no elevator).
4. Physical limitations
5. Psychological or spiritual challenges (possibly including anger at the pastor, the congregation, or God)
6. Lack of interest
7. Other

C. Do you listen to religious radio broadcasts? If so, which ones, and what meaning do they have for you?

D. Do you watch religious television programs? If so, which ones? How are they meaningful for you?

E. What are some of your favorite hymns? How are they meaningful for you?

F. In which church groups or activities were or are you active?

Communion assistant	Lector
Usher	Altar guild member
Adult choir member	Soloist/choir
Sunday school teacher	Church council member
Quilting group member	Women's group member
Circle member	Prayer chain member
Youth group advisor	Parish visitor
Senior adult group member	Senior advisory committee member

Committees ______________________________

Church office volunteer ______________________

Other ______________________________

III. Scripture

A. What are some of your favorite Bible passages and stories? What meaning do they have for you?
B. What are your favorite parts of the Bible? Why are they favorites?
C. How often do you read the Bible?
D. Do you read daily devotional books and other spiritual literature? If so, which ones? How are they meaningful?

IV. Prayer

A. What are your preferred forms of prayer?
   1. Personal free-flowing prayer
   2. Prayers during worship services
   3. Memorized bedtime prayer
   4. Music: hymns, choral, instrumental
   5. Lord's Prayer
   6. Table grace
   7. Silent prayer
   8. Printed prayers
   9. Other
B. For what do you pray?
C. How often do you pray?
   1. All day
   2. Several times a day
   3. Once a day
   4. Only in an emergency or crisis
   5. Never

V. Sacraments

A. How old were you when you were baptized?
B. What was your parents' denomination when you were baptized?
C. What have you been told about your baptism, or what do you remember?
   1. Were you baptized in church or at home?
   2. Where did you live at the time?
   3. Who were your sponsors?
   4. Did you wear a special baptismal gown?
D. What does it mean to you that you are baptized?
E. Have there been especially significant baptisms in your family or among your friends? What made them significant?
F. When and where did you receive your first communion?
G. What does Holy Communion mean to you?
H. How often do you like to receive Holy Communion?

VI. God

A. How do you view God? As a God of:
   1. Love and mercy
   2. Anger and judgment
   3. Distance and hiddenness
   4. Peace and joy
   5. Promise and hope
   6. Control
B. What role has God had throughout your life?
C. Is your relationship with God:
   1. Close and personal?
   2. Occasional, in which you turn to God once in a while?
   3. Nonexistent?
D. Do you sometimes become angry with God? If so, when? How do you feel about being angry with God?
E. How did you serve God before you retired?
F. If you are retired, how do you serve God in your retirement?

VII. Jesus

A. Who is Jesus for you?
   1. Friend
   2. Comforter
   3. Shepherd
   4. Savior
   5. Teacher
   6. Other
B. To what extent is Jesus a source of comfort and strength for you?
   1. A great deal
   2. Quite a bit
   3. Some
   4. Not at all
C. Do you believe that God forgives your sins through Jesus' death and resurrection?
D. Do you have past or current sins that trouble you?
   1. If so, would you like to talk about them with the pastor?
   2. When will you call the pastor to make an appointment to discuss them?

VIII. Meaning

A. What were the most meaningful religious events and spiritual experiences in your childhood? What meaning did they have for you?
B. What have been the most meaningful religious events and spiritual experiences in your adulthood? What meaning did they have for you?
C. Do you have a reason to get up each day? If so, what is it?
D. How has the meaning of your life changed over the years?

E. Does your faith give meaning to your life? If so, how?
F. What is your philosophy of life?
G. Do you find meaning in illness, stress, and affliction? If so, what have you found?
H. How do you cope with illness, stress, and affliction?
    1. Become depressed
    2. Give up
    3. Shed tears
    4. Pray laments ("Why me?" "How long?")
    5. Pray for strength and comfort
    6. Trust in God
    7. Seek options
    8. Other
I. Have you experienced meaningful dreams, religious or nonreligious? If so, describe a dream and its meanings.
J. How do you meaningfully contribute to the well-being of others?
    1. Volunteer work, such as ______________________________
    2. Doing good deeds for others, such as ____________________
    3. Sharing my creative expertise with others, such as ________
K. Do you feel as much pleasure in life as you used to? Do the things that used to make you happy still do so? If not, how often do you feel in a low mood?
    1. How do you deal with a low mood?
    2. Have you recently experienced changes in your sleep patterns or eating habits?
    3. Do you feel now that life is worth living? If not, please call your pastor or a professional counselor.

IX. Perspective on Aging

A. What are the best things about your age now?
B. What do you hope for as you grow older?
C. What is the most difficult part of growing old?
D. What do you hope that you never have to give up?
E. What is your secret to living a long life?
F. What is the biggest change you have experienced in your lifetime?
G. If you could share words of wisdom with younger people, what would you share?

X. Death and Afterlife

A. What significant deaths have you experienced among your family and friends?

B. Have you had any near-death experiences? If so, describe them and the meaning they had for you.
C. Do you fear death?
   1. If so, what do you fear?
   2. Do you feel comfortable calling the pastor to make an appointment to talk about your fears?
   3. If so, when will you call your pastor?
D. What do you want to do before you die?
E. Is there something important you would like to say to someone before you die? What? Can you tell this person? When?
F. What is your view of the afterlife?
G. If you believe in heaven, what do you look forward to there?
H. As you look ahead to your inevitable death, which of the following would you prefer in your last days?
   1. Family presence
   2. Close friends' presence
   3. Pastoral presence
   4. Being alone
   5. Holy Communion
   6. Holy Scripture
   7. Recorded music, such as ___

   (Call the pastor and make an appointment to discuss your preferences.)
I. Have you planned your funeral and burial?
   1. If you have, communicate your plans to your family and the pastor.
   2. If not, would you like the pastor's help with this task? If so, call and make an appointment.
J. Do you have a living will?
   1. If so, do you know where it is?
   2. Have you shared it with your family and physician?
   3. If not, would you like help making a living will?

XI. Christian Decision-making

A. Does your faith help you make decisions? If so, how?
B. How often do you try to discover what God wants you to do when you have decisions to make?
   1. Often
   2. Sometimes
   3. Seldom
   4. Never
C. What most strongly influences your decision-making?
D. What types of decisions do you allow others to help you make?
E. What types of decisions do you want to make by yourself?

XII. Peace

A. How often do you experience inner peace?
   1. Always
   2. Frequently
   3. It comes and goes
   4. Seldom
   5. Never

B. When do you experience inner peace?

C. If you do not experience inner peace, what hinders you from experiencing it?

XIII. Faith

A. What nurtures your faith?
   1. Worship attendance
   2. Bible reading
   3. Prayer
   4. Pastoral visitation
   5. Spiritual Journey Exercise for Individuals (appendix A)
   6. Holy Communion
   7. Devotional reading
   8. The sharing of my faith
   9. Religious art and music

XIV. Religious Questions

A. Do you have religious questions which you would like to discuss?

B. Call your pastor to make an appointment to discuss your questions.

APPENDIX B

Internet Web Sites on Aging

Age Wave	www.agewave.com
Ageless Design, Inc.	www.agelessdesign.com
Alzheimer's Association	www.alz.org
Alzheimer Page, Washington University, St. Louis, Mo.	www.biostat.wustl.edu/alzheimer
American Association of Retired Persons	www.aarp.org
American Association of Homes and Services for the Aging	www.aahsa.org
American Health Assistance Foundation	www.ahaf.org
American Society on Aging	www.asaging.org
Area Agencies on Aging	www.aoa.dhhs.gov/aoa/webres/area-agn.htm
Arthritis Foundation	www.arthritis.org
Assisted Living Federation of America	www.alfa.org
Center for Aging, Religion, and Spirituality at Luther Seminary, St. Paul, Minnesota	www.luthersem.edu/cars
Center for the Advanced Study of Aging Services	www.cssr21.socwel.berkeley.edu/aging

Council for Jewish Elderly	www.cje.net
Deaf and Disabled Telecommunications Program	www.ddtp.org
Dementia Web, London	http://dementia.ion.ucl.ac.uk
Elderhostel	www.elderhostel.org
Family Caregiver Alliance	www.caregiver.org
Forum on Religion, Spirituality, and Aging of the American Society on Aging	www.asaging.org/forsa.html
Internet Mental Health	www.mentalhealth.com
National Council on the Aging, Inc.	www.shs.net/ncoa/ncoa.htm
National Federation of Interfaith Volunteer Caregivers	www.nfivc.org
National Institute on Aging	www.nih.gov/nia
Senior Law	www.seniorlaw.com
Social Security Administration	www.ssa.gov
Stephen Ministries	www.stephenministries.org
Symposium on Ministry with the Aging	http://207.15.178.1/jubilee/symposium
United States Administration on Aging	www.aoa.dhhs.gov

NOTES

Chapter 1

1. Stephen Ministries (2045 Innerbelt Business Center Drive, St. Louis, Mo. 63114-5765, 314-428-2600) provides a training program for congregational lay visitors.

Chapter 2

1. Paul Tillich, *The Courage To Be* (New Haven: Yale University Press, 1952), 50.

Chapter 3

1. Sue V. Saxon and Mary Jean Etten, *Physical Change and Aging: A Guide for Helping Professionals* (New York: Tiresias Press), 372-73.

Chapter 4

1. United States Administration on Aging, "Profiles of Older Americans: 1998" (http://www.aoa.dhhs.gov/aoa/stats/profile/), 2.
2. "Profiles of Older Americans," 4.
3. "Profiles of Older Americans," 4.
4. "Profiles of Older Americans," 4.
5. "Profiles of Older Americans," 4.

Chapter 5

Tillich, *The Courage To Be*, 190.

Chapter 8

1. "Profiles of Older Americans," 2.
2. "Profiles of Older Americans," 3.
3. "Profiles of Older Americans," 3.
4. "Profiles of Older Americans," 2.

Chapter 9

1. Materials available through the Association of Lutheran Older Adults, Valparaiso University, Valparaiso, Ind. 46383. Phone 800-930-2562. E-mail: aloa1@juno.com

Chapter 10

1. *Lutheran Book of Worship* (Minneapolis and Philadelphia: Augsburg Publishing House and Board of Publication, Lutheran Church in America, 1978), 206.

2. Anderson Funeral Home, Montevideo, Minn., "Service of Remembrance" bulletin, Dec. 6, 1997, 3.

3. Anderson Funeral Home, "Service of Remembrance" bulletin, 4.

Chapter 11

1. Mary H. Brahe (music) and Helen Taylor (words), "Bless This House," copyright (c) 1927, 1932 by Boosey & Co. Ltd.; copyright renewed by Boosey & Hawkes, Inc. Recordings of "Bless This House" and other music for this service can be obtained from the Public Radio Music Source, phone 800-756-8742.

BIBLIOGRAPHY

"Aging and the Older Adult." Social Statements of the Lutheran Church in America. Adopted July 1978 by the Ninth Biennial LCA Convention, Chicago, Ill.

Althaus, Paul. *The Theology of Martin Luther.* Philadelphia: Fortress, 1975.

Batzka, David L. "Instruction Manual for the Older Adult Church Survey Project." National Benevolent Association, Division of Social and Health Services, Christian Church (Disciples of Christ) Department of Services to Congregations (n.d.).

Black, Helen K. "Wasted Lives and the Hero Grown Old: Personal Perspectives of Spirituality by Aging Men." *Journal of Religious Gerontology* 9 (1995): 35-48.

Bornkamm, Gunther. *Jesus of Nazareth.* New York: Harper & Row, 1975.

Davidson, Glen W. *Living With Dying.* Minneapolis: Augsburg, 1975.

Ellor, James W., and Sheldon S. Tobin. "Beyond Visitation: Ministries With The Homebound Elderly." *Journal of Pastoral Care*, 39, no. 1 (1985): 12-21.

Feifel, Herman, ed. *The Meaning of Death.* New York: McGraw-Hill, 1959.

Fitchett, George. "A Model of Spiritual Assessment." *CareGiver Journal of College of Chaplains*, no. 5 (1988): 144-154.

———. *Assessing Spiritual Needs: A Guide for Caregivers.* Minneapolis: Augsburg, 1993.

Frerichs, Wendell. "What It Meant to Grow Old in Biblical Times." Lecture, Geriatric Pastoral Care Institute, Luther Seminary, St. Paul, Minn., July 16, 1996.

Gillespie, V. Bailey. *The Experience of Faith.* Birmingham, Ala.: Religious Education Press, 1988.

Gray, Robert M., and David O. Moberg. *The Church and the Older Person.* Grand Rapids: Eerdmans, 1977.

Haight, Barbara K. "Life Review: A Method for Pastoral Counseling: Part I." *Journal of Religion and Aging*, no. 5 (1989): 17-29.

Harris, J. Gordon. *Biblical Perspectives on Aging: God and the Elderly*. Philadelphia: Fortress, 1987.

Hays, Edward. *Prayers for the Domestic Church: A Handbook for Worship in the Home*. Leavenworth, Kans.: Forest of Peace Publishing, 1979.

Heinecken, Martin J., and Ralph R. Hellerich. *The Church's Ministry with Older Adults: A Theological Basis*. New York: Lutheran Church in America, 1976.

Hiltner, Seward. *Toward a Theology of Aging*. New York: Human Sciences Press, 1979.

Hulme, William E. Vintage Years: Growing Older With Meaning and Hope. Philadelphia: Westminster, 1986.

Ivy, Steven S. "Pastoral Diagnosis as Pastoral Caring." *Journal of Pastoral Care*, 42, no. 1 (1988): 81-89.

Kelsey, Morton T. *Afterlife: The Other Side of Dying*. New York: Paulist, 1979.

Kimble, Melvin A., ed., with James W. Ellor, Susan H. McFadden, and James J. Seeber. *Aging, Religion, and Spirituality: A Handbook.* Minneapolis: Fortress, 1995.

Kimble, Melvin, and James W. Ellor. "Logotherapy: An Overview." White Paper, National-Louis University and American Society on Aging, 1989.

Maletta, Gabe. "Aging Changes in the Neural System: Normal vs. Pathological." Lecture, Geriatric Pastoral Care Institute, Luther Seminary, July 22, 1996.

McSherry, Elisabeth. "Modernization of the Clinical Science of Chaplaincy." *CareGiver Journal of College of Chaplains*, no. 4 (1987): 1-13.

McSherry, Elisabeth, and Henry Nichols. *Spiritual Profile Assessment Manual*, Version 1.0. West Roxbury, Mass.: Veterans Administration Medical Center (n.d.).

Missinne, Leo, and Judy Willeke-Kay. "Reflections on the Meaning of Life in Old Age." *Journal of Religion and Aging*, 1, no. 4 (1985): 43-58.

Moberg, David O. "Subjective Measures of Well-being." *Review of Religious Research*. 25, no. 4 (1984).

Occasional Services: A Companion to the Lutheran Book of Worship. Minneapolis and Philadelphia: Augsburg Publishing House and the Board of Publication, Lutheran Church in America, 1982.

Pierce, James, and Larry VandeCreek. "Life Values Assessment Database and Profiles." *CareGiver Journal of the College of Chaplains*, no. 8 (1991): 30-38.

Potok, Chaim. *My Name Is Asher Lev*. Greenwich, Conn.: Fawcett, 1972.

Ramshaw, Elaine, and Don S. Browning, eds. *Ritual and Pastoral Care*. Philadelphia: Fortress, 1987.

Rando, Therese A. *Grief, Dying, and Death: Clinical Interventions for Caregivers*. Champaign, Ill.: Research Press, 1984.

Richards, Marty, and Sam Seicol. "The Challenge of Maintaining Spiritual Connectedness for Persons Institutionalized with Dementia." *Journal of Religious Gerontology*, no. 7 (1991): 27-39.

Richardson, Alan, ed. *A Theological Word Book of the Bible*. New York: Macmillan, 1977.

Sapp, Stephen. *Full of Years: Aging and the Elderly in the Bible and Today*. Nashville: Abingdon, 1987.

Saxon, Sue V., and Mary Jean Etten. *Physical Change and Aging*. New York: Tiresias Press, 1994.

Seicol, Richard. "The Challenge of Maintaining Spiritual Connectedness for Persons Institutionalized with Dementia." *Journal of Religious Gerontology*, 7, no. 3 (1991).

Shorter Book of Blessings. International Commission on English in the Liturgy (Joint Commission of Catholic Bishops' Conferences). New York: Catholic Book Publishing Co., 1990.

Simmons, Henry C. "Teach Us To Pray: Pastoral Care of the New Nursing Home Resident." *Journal of Pastoral Care*, 45, no. 2 (1991): 169-175.

Thibault, Jane M., James W. Ellor, and F. Ellen Netting. "A Conceptual Framework for Assessing the Spiritual Functioning and Fulfillment of Older Adults in Long-Term Care Settings." *Journal of Religious Gerontology*, no. 7 (1991): 29-45.

Tillich, Paul. *The Courage To Be*. New Haven: Yale University Press, 1952.

Tobin, Sheldon S., James W. Ellor, and Susan M. Anderson-Ray. *Enabling the Elderly*. New York: University of New York Press, 1986.

Uhlman, Jerry, and Paul D. Steinke. "Pastoral Care for the Institutionalized Elderly: Determining And Responding To Their Need." *Journal of Pastoral Care*, 39, no. 1 (1985): 22-30.

United States Administration on Aging. "Profiles of Older Americans: 1998." Internet: http://www.aoa.dhhs.gov/aoa/stats/profile

CD-ROM INSTRUCTIONS

This edition of *Understanding the Senior Adult* is packaged with a cross-platform CD-ROM which contains the following materials:

- Downloadable RTF files of all appendix materials that can be read and manipulated in most word processing programs, regardless of platform;
- Downloadable PDF files containing all the forms from the book appendices that can be read using Adobe Acrobat Reader;
- Adobe Acrobat Reader for reading the PDF files for both Macintosh and PC computers.

All of the files on the disk are accessible by computers equipped with CD-ROM drives meeting the systems requirements listed below.

INSTRUCTIONS FOR INSTALLING ADOBE ACROBAT READER 4.0

Windows

System Requirements:

- i486 or Pentium processor-based personal computer
- Microsoft Windows 95, Windows 98, or Windows NT with Service Task 3 or later
- 8 MB of RAM on Windows 95 and Windows 98 (16 MB recommended)
- 10 MB of available hard disk space
- Additional 50 MB of hard disk space for Asian fonts (optional)

Installing and Uninstalling:

- Uninstall Acrobat Reader 3.x using the uninstaller available through the start menu (if necessary)
- Make sure you have at least 10 MB of available disk space
- Install Acrobat Reader 4.0 – ar 40eng.exe by following screen prompts

Note: If you uninstall Acrobat 3.x or Acrobat Reader 3.x after installing Acrobat Reader 4.0, you will need to reinstall Acrobat Reader 4.0 for it to work properly.

After installation is complete, double-click on any of the .pdf files to view the contents and print as desired

Macintosh

System Requirements:

- Apple Power Macintosh computer
- Apple System Software version 7.1.2 or later
- 4.5 MB of RAM available to Acrobat Reader (6.5 MB recommended)
- 8 MB of available hard disk space
- Additional 50 MB of hard disk space for Asian Fonts (optional)

Installing and uninstalling:

- Uninstall Acrobat Reader 3.x if desired.
- Make sure you have at least 10 MB of available disk space
- Double-click on the Acrobat Reader 4.0 installer and follow the screen prompts

After installation is complete, double-click on any of the .pdf files to view the contents and print as desired.